Cheating

Is

Not

Cheating

Naiym "Wolf" Dingle

Written & Edited by Naiym "Wolf" Dingle

Book Design & Cover by TahGee Williams

Book Formatting by J. Cerrone Smith

ISBN 978-1-7347648-0-2

First Step Marketing LLC

Philadelphia, PA

Table of Contents

Pre-Chapters:

- The Mission – *4*
- The Wolf Has Spoken – *7*
- Thank You – *9*
- Before You Read – *10*
- As You Read – *12*

Chapters:

Chapter 1 – Cheating is Not Cheating – *14*

Chapter 2 – What is Cheating? – *21*

Chapter 3 – Men vs. Women Cheating – *25*

Chapter 4 – Can a Man Commit Capital Behavior? – *41*

Chapter 5 – A Woman Committing Manslaughter – *49*

Chapter 6 – Manslaughter vs. Capital: Understanding the Terms – *56*

Chapter 7 – Intent Changes Everything: Explaining My Points – *83*

Chapter 8 – Stop Ignoring the Double-Standard – *94*

Chapter 9 – Pride & Ego – *101*

Chapter 10 – His Weak Ego Made Him Do It; Her Strong Pride Couldn't Let It Go – *119*

Chapter 11 – Should you Forgive? – *170*

Chapter 12 – How to Forgive – *180*

Chapter 13 – Things to Take With You – *192*

The Mission

As a kid, I always knew in my heart that I would serve a purpose bigger than I could imagine. It's been my goal since a child to have an impact that would change the world. While most kids saw the world as something big, I've always seen it as something small, small enough that one person could do something to impact the world in its entirety.

Overcoming everything that I endured during my upbringing, dating back to the day I was born, was to prepare me for something great. I came into this world with the odds stacked against me, and I have spent every day since then on a mission to beat the odds. Most people enter the world on a mission; I entered the world with a mission. I always knew I was blessed; it was evident by the number of blessings that were bestowed upon me, even in the face of adversity and constant times of hardship. Almost to a point where I knew I was being guided and guarded by a higher power.

I didn't grow up financially fortunate, but fortunately enough, I was never put into a predicament that I couldn't handle. I didn't know what my purpose would be, but as I reflect, I can vividly recollect the series of events in my life that lead and prepared me for this moment.

I was sent here with a message and a gift. The message is in my ability to communicate, and the gift is in my ability to understand people. Through these words, I deliver the message, and with this gift, I can heal by helping people understand themselves.

If you've made it this far, I think it's safe to say,

Mission accomplished!

The Wolf Has Spoken

My name is Naiym Dingle. I am most referred to as "Wolf." I am currently 27 years old as I write this to you today. I spent the vast majority of my life up to this point, trying to follow my passions and align with my purpose in an attempt to find myself. In doing so, I ventured off into multiple endeavors, doing what I thought I wanted to do and, in some cases, doing things in an attempt to please others.

Through these failed attempts to find myself, I arrived at the realization that life isn't about finding yourself. We are born who we are. Life is about understanding yourself and accepting yourself. If you're going through life with no understanding of who you are, you'll always feel lost, confused, and out of place. I learned that through my many different experiences.

So, my advice to you is, don't go through life seeking the approval or validation of others because others can't validate what they don't understand. It's only essential that you understand. Live freely and be who YOU are!

Thank You

To everyone who has helped me along this journey through conversations, inspirations, and experiences! I send my deepest love and appreciation. Thank You

Before You Read

STOP! Before you even begin to read this book, there are a few things I want to establish right here! This is not a book on equality or human rights. This is not a book on who's right or who's wrong. This is not a book on men vs. women. This is not a book on your personal experiences. This is not a book on how we wish things could be.

This is a book on how things are. This is a book based on authentic human behavioral studies, tendencies, and observations in and out of relationships, as well as transitioning between relationships. If you're looking for a book with a narrative that's depicting a perfect world, with perfect people and perfect relationships, then put this book down and pick up a book in the fairytale section. This book is written solely for the men and women in the world who are seeking understanding about one another and open to receive it. This book is written in efforts of providing the truth to establishing and maintaining happiness in or out of a relationship, through understanding and being understood.

Most importantly! This book is written to save a nation of people from suffering behind the views and opinions of a society that has convinced people to hate their reality.

As You Read

Take notes if necessary. This book is going to open some minds, close some doors, and spark some controversy. All of this is great because this is a conversation that needs to be had if we are to restore the nature in relationships, by replacing fantasy with reality.

Put your personal views, feelings, emotions, and experiences to the side and allow yourself to be openminded to receiving new information. If you are reading this book in attempts to gain understanding, you must develop and maintain an open mind. If you're reading this book to rebuttal, then be sure to cross-examine your own point of view in the process.

To grasp new concepts, you have to be open to challenging what you think you already know. You should also understand that the first thing you were taught isn't always right. The truth is, there are no universal laws that can validate personal perspectives, so all we have is our experiences, which makes it difficult to challenge our views! But if we are to survive in a world of people filled with opinions, we must be open to understanding the perspectives of others.

Chapter 1

Cheating Is Not Cheating

I know it's often said that you shouldn't judge a book by the cover or, in this case, the title, but with this book, that's what I want you to do! Judge this book by its title. Go ahead, read it out loud to yourself, take a deep breath, and read it out loud again, tap somebody close to you, and say it to them.

How does it sound when you say it? Cheating is not cheating. Does it seem rational or absurd? How do you perceive this statement? Are you reading it with an open mind or an emotional heart? This title is a true statement. Stick with me all way through as I set out to help you understand and explain why it is so. Cheating is NOT cheating. I find myself making

14

this statement a lot, and every time I say it, I see some eyebrows raise, some head-scratching, or I hear murmuring.

Honestly, not many people agree with me initially, and I find myself engaged in a back and forth conversation discussing the different perspectives. Concluding every discussion, I learn that it's not that people don't agree with the statement, but more so, their perception of the statement isn't aligned with the reality of the statement.

Literally, 90% of the open discussions start with two different perspectives only to result in the person I'm having a discussion with arriving at an understanding of my point of view. The more I make the statement, the more I find myself having these discussions, whether it be on a street corner or on my social media platform. I've come to realize that there's something about this statement that sparks outrage and controversy. Now as much as I would love to have these discussions with every single individual on this planet that wants to challenge my perspective, I just don't have the time. So, I've decided to write this book. This book gives the people around the world that have different perspectives an inside look at my point of view.

When I say cheating is not cheating, it's not to say that cheating is appropriate or acceptable on any level. It's me saying that cheating is not cheating, it's not something you can generalize because each scenario is different and deserving of a different but appropriate punishment. Everyone views cheating with a different point of view because everyone has a personal definition of what's considered to be cheating.

So, to generalize, cheating is like generalizing a crime. Yes, all crimes are illegal, but not all crimes are subjected to the same punishment. You're not going to see a criminal that was arrested for stealing a candy bar face the same charges as someone who robbed a bank at gunpoint. Are both of them considered criminals? Of course. Are both going to spend the same amount of time in prison if found guilty on their charges? No.

The same analogy applies in regard to cheating. The main reason for this is, all humans experience a different emotional reaction when they're cheated on. This means there's no generalized way to look at it. What one person may find to be ok another may find to be unacceptable. One man or woman may feel it is unacceptable to go on lunch dates with a co-worker of the opposite sex while another man or woman may view it as harmless, as long as no ill intent went into the lunch date. There are people out here in open relationships and engaging in an activity known as "swinging," there are also people out here that if they were to catch their spouse with someone else, they'd start swinging to initiate a fight.

These examples are transparent across the board. What one may be ok with another may not. It's important to have a discussion with a potential partner during the dating stages regarding your personal view on cheating. This way, both of you have an understanding of what behaviors may cause turmoil between the two of you. Do note that if someone has an issue with certain behaviors that you are unwilling to change or vice versa, you and that person may not be right for one another. No need to force it, no need to judge each other, there's someone out there for each of you even if it doesn't work out for you two together.

A lot of relationships begin without discussing the boundaries of what one another considers to be cheating, and you'll see these relationships suffer because of it. This type of lack of effective communication is the root of a lot of unnecessary heartaches and avoidable confusion. Once confusion stirs up in a relationship from one person feeling like they were cheated on due to there being no set boundaries as to what one finds to be appropriate, the relationship will face constant turmoil and battle with trust issues.

This can all be avoided if you lay on the table what you are ok with and what will cause problems. Making the assumption that cheating is cheating and that everyone views cheating the way that you do will have you feeling out of place in the world of dating, causing you to feel alienated on the planet of love. I know all of this is raising you to ask yourself if cheating is not cheating, then what is considered to be cheating?

Chapter 2

What Is Cheating?

The truth is you set the standard for what you want to consider as cheating, the reality to that truth is, the standard you set is just your perspective and not everyone else's. Each and every individual roaming this earth is entitled to their own opinion creating their own view. The controversy is created when people project their personal perspective about cheating on to the world, creating judgment toward other people for not sharing the same perspective. Cheating is viewed differently based on one's personal preference, as stated above.

I'll use myself, for example, I am not going to consider my girlfriend texting another man on the same level as I would if she were to have sex with the guy whom she's texting. Can texting lead to sex? Hell yes! But I base what I consider to be cheating off of the intent behind the actions. If my girlfriend were texting a guy having a meaningless conversation about their shared interest, I am ok with that. I am not ok with my girlfriend using text messages to create arrangements to link up and have sex, lol. There are some guys out here that'll disagree with me and say they don't even want their woman having the phone number of another man who's not their family member. At one point in my life, I thought just as they do. Until I was forced to ask myself, "What is cheating?"

Honestly, I still have yet to successfully answer the question as to what I consider cheating because what I found inappropriate in one relationship, I found myself completely ok with in the next. Each relationship is helping me to increase the boundaries of what I consider to be cheating.

With that being said, it's not for me to judge them, and it's not for them to judge me, it's for everyone to understand that we all have different views on what we consider to be appropriate or inappropriate in our relationship. Cheating is viewed differently from gender, age, race, ethnicity, marital status, and, most importantly, experience. I don't think it's possible to have everyone arrive at one concise agreement as to what cheating is considered to be. We'd have a better shot at creating one political party between the democrats and republicans or getting north and south Korea to come together and unite as one. Impossible.

Arriving at one concise agreement may be impossible, but I do feel like this book can serve as a guideline to enlighten you all on how cheating can be viewed based on the intent behind it. Similar to how there are different level offenses to crime. There are different level offenses to cheating. Keep an open mind as you read.

Chapter 3

Men vs. Women Cheating

Relationships tend to end for various reasons but none more infamous than CHEATING. It's some unwritten statistical fact that cheating is the leading cause of a relationship coming to an end. Somehow, even with everybody understanding this being the societal deal-breaker, it still doesn't stop it from happening, nor does it have an impact on slowing the rate of cheating down. It's almost to a point where it is utterly disrespectful to your relationship to cheat, knowing the weight it holds on destroying your relationship.

I like to compare the consciousness of cheating to a criminal with crimes. No one actually thinks about the aftermath while in the act. If anything, it's a

25

distant thought until you're in the process of being caught or caught already. Like I can guarantee you that you've never heard, nor will you ever hear a criminal say, "Yeah, I know I'll get caught and spend ten years of my life in jail" and still commit the crime. Where does that happen at? Nowhere! It's the exact same concept with cheating. Rarely is the aftermath or consequences ever thought about, let alone considered in the decision-making process. I understand that in some instances, premeditation plays a factor. It also increases the level of offense, because one would argue that a conscious decision was made to commit a crime regardless of the potential punishment.

Even with all that being said, NO ONE thinks they will be caught. If premeditation resulted in someone factoring in the potential of being caught, there's a high chance; they wouldn't do it. You'd have to arrive at "Fuck It" to go through with any act knowing you'll face potential consequences, I'm just saying. Notice how up to this point I didn't specify who cheats I just generally spoke on cheating. I did that because I feel as though cheating isn't done more by one specific gender how-ever, I do think that the way it's done by men/women differs behind the intent. There's no real justification for cheating for either party, but I will break down the differences between men and women cheating based on motive and intent.

Even with the end result being the same, the punishment should be different, just saying. It's like manslaughter vs. capital murder. I would consider a man cheating to fall under the manslaughter category if we had to go to relationship court for how the relationship was killed. Now before you go off the deep end or develop an opinion, hear me out. After hearing me out, feel free to develop your own opinion...ok? Deal!

If you think about manslaughter, typically, it is the criminal justice system giving you a lesser time for an offense not to be considered extremely heinous. A punishment that puts you in prison for some time but never for life. The reason being, the prosecutor, judge, or jury didn't feel that the crime was committed with malice or premeditated intent. It's like one of those by mistake things or something that occurs in the spur of the moment with no prior thought. This comparison can be made to how men cheat.

Now, wait! I know you're probably wondering how I plan to piece together murder with cheating. Step away from the specifics of what I am saying and just understand the analogy of cheating being the murderer of relationships. Back to my point, A man typically cheats in the spur of the moment, it typically has no sentimental value, and it's not something he plans to pursue. It's literally just an experience! I can guarantee you that a man doesn't think of what he's risking as he's getting ready to tear down some new pussy, it's just not something that crosses his mind. No matter how long y'all been together, it doesn't matter the amount of love the two of you share or the status of the relationship at the time. If a guy is tempted with an opportunity to cheat and he acts on it, he's not doing so with the intent to mess up what he has at home.

Now I know by now you all are sitting here thinking, "how isn't a man trying to mess up what he has at home if he's cheating on the person he is claiming to love?" I'm here to tell you that LOVE has absolutely nothing to do with his decision.

Consequences may become a thought when he's finished (For however long it lasts). He's more than likely to leave everything associated with the experience inside the condom he came in (hopefully, he used one). This applies to any and all women that he sleeps with. They can't be looked at as anything more than an experience.

The reason I make the comparison to manslaughter is that seldomly does a man cheating actually end the relationship forever. There'd have to be indisputable circumstances that force a female to move on because, in most cases, she's more than likely to hear him out and take him back. Sounds stupid, right? Actually, it's not because, in most cases, women develop the fear of being cheated on again after being cheated on the first time. This fear isn't limited to their current relationship. It carries on with them throughout their life when they think about it long-term. Even when it's merely a thought. The thought of them moving on and being cheated on by their new partner is what keeps them in bondage to their current relationship, hoping that it never happens again while fearing to start over.

Women invest differently when in a relationship. Women can literally see a future in anybody they deal with, which makes things hard for them because they tend to chase potential in most cases. This fault in women is often taken advantage of by men and is the reason why women are more than likely to forgive a man that cheats on them even if he cheats multiple times. A woman is more likely to assume all men cheat so she might as well stay with the one she's been with for however long as opposed to starting over and repeating the cycle.

This is why I say a man cheating is more likely to fall under the category of manslaughter. Yes, it affects the relationship, and it might birth insecurities that last forever, but it never ends the relationship completely. A man would have to be a repeat offender beyond explanation for a woman to terminate the relationship. See, women will put up with a man's nonsense for as long as they can justify it, but the moment they have no more grounds to stand on, neither will the relationship.

Isn't it outrageous that women will put a man on trial for cheating and then show up as his attorney in the eyes of the public! Crazy right? I know!! But I guess we can accredit that to a female's nature. A woman is always willing to hear a man out after he cheats, do you want to know why? Because women are curious, and they require closure! They have to get to the bottom of why? Why did you do it? Why did you lie? What was the role they played in your decision-making process, and was there something they could've done to prevent it? This need for closure is how a man can plead his case, ask for forgiveness, and in most cases, receive it. This is why I consider it manslaughter because even after committing such an action, a man is still given a second chance, it doesn't matter the details included in the second chance the facts are the relationship survived. It wasn't killed by the man slaughtering some pussy! Ha-ha-ha-ha-ha-ha! Ok, ok! I'm done with the jokes. I just had to get that out.

On another note, a female's act of cheating is viewed as capital behavior that will, in most cases, receive capital punishment in the execution of the relationship or a lifetime of being accused and never being forgiven. Now I know what the women are probably thinking by now if they haven't already put the book down. "He's biased for men. How could he think he understands women and how we think? Who does he think he is? We need a female's perspective. Of course, he will say that because he's a man! BLAH BLAH BLAH!"

But before you go on bashing my views take a step back to at least attempt to understand or follow where I'm going with this.

A female is more respectful of her body and treats her goods in a more sacred manner than a man does with his. Women want sex to mean something, so they'll rather not sleep with anyone as opposed to sleeping with just with any and everybody. Most importantly, there has to be some type of connection beyond physical attraction to the person they're given themselves to, ESPECIALLY if they're running the risk of destroying their relationship. A female's act of cheating is almost ALWAYS premeditated even if its spur of the moment she stills finds the time to ask herself if it's worth it. A woman will even create the time to imagine life with the dude she's cheating with and if he could provide her with the life she wants or a lifestyle better than the one she's currently living in her current relationship. Women all across the world can attempt to deny this. My facts remain the same for all the women following where I'm going with this.

The status of the relationship also plays a major factor in a female deciding to cheat or if cheating is worth the consequences that may arise from it if caught. Understand that a woman has needs. If all of her needs are being fulfilled, she will not cheat at all! Women require security in a multitude of ways, and if she can find all of that in one man, she's not giving that up for anything in the world.

The only problem with that is women have too many needs often not found in just one man, and most of them don't realize they have this need until they're exposed to it. A female can be 100% happy with the ten things a man provides her. These ten things may be all she ever wanted based on her understanding of what she wanted until she's exposed to something else that enhances her desires, enticing her to think she wants something else.

As children, women are taught life is a fairytale, and there is a man out there that will cater to their every need. Combine these thoughts with curiosity and a desire for more, then BAM, her happiness is tampered with. She's viewing the lack of the relationship as opposed to what she actually has. Which again only becomes an issue because women struggle most in determining what they want.

Don't believe me? Ask a female what she wants to eat for dinner, better yet ask her to tell you ten things she wants that'll make her life complete! I bet she either names 50 or can't make it past five. See, when you force a female to think about what they want, it creates imaginary borders on their thought process, which makes them feel limited to whatever they say they want, which in tune makes deciding a million times harder. Bring it all way back to their premeditated decision to cheat. If a female can identify something distinctive in the man they decide to cheat with that's lacking in their current spouse, it gives them self-justification as to why they did it and why it was worth it. No matter the void being filled, it can be related to money, time, or love and affection. A female is only going to cheat with someone who fills a void in bridging the gap to the perfect happiness that they desire. Women need self-justification because it provides them with personal grounds to stand on.

So, in any event, they are caught they can live with knowing they chose to chase bigger happiness as opposed to not giving it a try. Even if the happiness woman seek is imaginary and only exist in a vulnerable state of mind, they can live with their decision because they thought it all the way through. For that, a woman cheating is considered to be a capital offense. If you think about it (Which she did) lmao and weigh in the actions, it was definitely premeditated, it was definitely intentional, and it definitely involved emotions.

For that, a man is most likely to never be able to forgive her. Even if a man decides to stay in the relationship, it is likely a dead situation. Resulting in the female trying to do all she can to revive it through a series of actions to prove her loyalty, remind him of all she's done for him, all the times she forgave him, in hopes of regaining his trust. In most cases, a woman will not be able to regain a man's trust after she's cheated on him. The reasons being is due to a man's pride, his ego, and his constant thought of another man having a part of his girlfriend.

It should also be noted that a man may also be aware of how a female came to her decision. Because of that, he develops a fear of the dude she cheated with reappearing, or he can't escape the thought of her actually planning to leave him for the other dude. All of these reasons stirred up creates the embarrassment a guy wouldn't want to bare in the eyes of the public or his friends and family if he were to take her back. This is why he would rather terminate the relationship completely. Even if he cheated fifty times and was forgiven each and every time. That wouldn't be enough of a solid ground for the relationship to stand on because, in his mind, none of the women he slept with meant anything. While this one guy she decided to cheat with actually meant something to her.

There is nothing a man fears more than his woman having a connection with another man! That's a fact.

Chapter 4

Can A Man Commit Capital Behavior?

I know after reading the last chapter, you're probably stuck asking yourself, "Can a man commit capital behavior?" or "What does a man have to do to deserve capital punishment?" To answer the question: YES, a man can commit a capital offense.

Still, men approach their capital behavior differently than women. Any man that invests in another woman beyond the experience in any way, shape, form, or fashion deserves capital punishment. Yes, I said it!

Now to further elaborate on what I mean by invest beyond the experience. Men will often spend money, take the time, and give all the energy necessary to create the experience. In some cases, the actions of a man may mimic all that he did in the beginning to gain the attention of his current girlfriend, but if you know men, you'll know that men tend to create routines and habits that can eventually become predictable.

Once a man finds a strategy that works to secure the hole, he's likely to reuse that same strategy over and over again, making minor changes to fit the interest of the woman in particular that he's trying to impress.

For Example: If his routine is to take a girl to dinner, a movie and cap it off with a parked car conversation as a first date, he will recreate this date over and over just making minor adjustments to the specifics like changing the location of the movie theater and switching restaurants.

Saying that helps understand why a woman shouldn't take it personally when a man takes a girl out while he's in a relationship. It means nothing, and it holds no sentimental value. Yes, I said it! It holds no sentimental value. It may have held value in the beginning when he first decided to take you on your first date, but shortly after, it became the strategy he would utilize when trying to get some new pussy.

I know most guys are reading this in agreeance as to these experiences, not having any sentimental value, which is why they see no issue in it. What's important for a man to understand is, a man doesn't determine the issue, the woman does, and this issue arises because although the man's view of it is harmless, a woman's view reflects the total opposite. There's sentiment involved from a woman's point of view because her dating experience with her man is what gained her interest in the first place. Making it impossible for her to view it any other way, leaving her with no choice but to associate the emotions she felt during their first date with the emotions that don't even exist in a man's re-creation of the experience.

The re-creation is a mirage. It looks like something, but it's nothing there, that won't stop a woman from applying emotion to the event telling herself that her man made the girl feel the same way he made her feel during their first date. Although she has no proof to validate it, she'll still experience the emotional trauma, not realizing that it's self-inflicted. There is a possibility that the girl on the date (we will just refer to her as "The Experience"), does develop emotions of feeling special during her experience because that's what the strategy is designed to do.

The strategy is created to help a man secure the hole in a short time-frame considering his window is small, and the task is big, well, unless she's just with it from the jump without any of the other antics, lol. Understand this; a man is going to do all that he has to do to secure the hole, nothing more and nothing less. Anything he does up until the point of getting the hole isn't considered an investment in his eyes. However, every moment spent with another woman is considered an investment in the eyes of his girlfriend.

A man's real investment starts after he gets the pussy. If he's still taking the experience on dates, creating time, investing energy, effort, or emotions, his actions deserve CAPITAL punishment! Because at this point, he's living a double life, in two relationships. The moment his investment becomes emotion-driven and no longer sex-driven, it is now a heinous offense. The only difference between what's considered to be game and what's considered to be the real thing is the emotional intent that fuels it. Yeah, a man may do the same things he did for his girlfriend, for ten other women, but those things stop after he has sex with them, whereas with his girlfriend, it's a never-ending number of things he's willing to do for her.

Most men follow the unwritten rule that if you're going to step out, don't allow it to affect home. Don't do it close to home, and DO NOT allow the experience to think she means anything to you that could impose a significant threat to your relationship. Men will do anything to abide by this unwritten rule, even if it means cutting off the experience like it's nothing. Most men understand the importance of not giving a girl one up on the woman he loves by making her think she's on equal playing fields or above his girlfriend in any way.

If there's a situation where a man's feelings get involved with the experience, and he's beginning to do things to protect her feelings like downplaying his relationship, his behavior is considered Capital and should be treated accordingly.

Another capital offense from a man can be dealing with an ex or a baby mama. There's no justification for these types of offenses because they are supposed to be dead situations that should never regain life. If they do, they were never dead. In the event a man is caught dealing with someone he's previously dealt with, it's in a woman's best interest to wash her hands with the situation or put on gloves and prepare for the mess. The absolute worst possible thing that a man can do under the statue of capital behavior involves coming home with an STD or a baby; those actions exhibit reckless behavior, whether emotions are involved or not.

Chapter 5

A Woman Committing Manslaughter

By now, you see that it is indeed possible for a man to commit Capital, and you are probably wondering if a woman can commit Manslaughter or, in this case, woman-slaughter, Ha-ha-ha! Lol! Alright, seriously, now. No more jokes.

The answer is: yes, of course! It'd be foolish to think that all women invested emotionally into every single man before or after sex. The only thing with woman slaughter is that the chances of it being committed are slim, and the chances of a man finding out are slimmer. Like, there's almost no way he'll find out! See, never underestimate a woman's sneaky intelligence, lying power, and ability to bury an event so deep in her mind that she can convince herself that the incident never happened. We call those the "To The Grave" moments. Believe it or not, every woman has or will have at some point in her life, a to the grave moment.

What is a to the grave moment you ask? Exactly what it sounds like, it's an event that a female will take to the grave unless there's indisputable evidence that can prove otherwise. These moments typically happen in the spur of the moment, during vulnerable or angry states of mind, mean nothing, often regretted, and it's just an experience, the same as it is for a man. The reason it must be taken to the grave by a woman is that a man wouldn't be willing to hear that, nor will he believe it, and she'd still end up receiving the capital punishment for her actions. The reason being, a man's ego wouldn't allow him to forgive her fully.

Women know and understand this, and by knowing this, it creates a fear so strong that a woman is willing to take that secret with her to the pine box. The reason it is so difficult to discover a female has a TTG moment (To The Grave Moment) is that there's less than a handful of people that are aware of this to the grave moment, and they typically have something of their own to lose if the secret were to get out. Why is that? Because women choose their conspirers wisely. Women only include people they can trust with their life or people they know something equally as devastating about just to level the playing field. This type of equal leverage decreases the chances of a loose end.

When you think about it, if men moved half as smart as women, their dumb asses wouldn't get caught. I know you are probably wondering when and how a woman's TTG moments occur. Well, women's TTG moments occur in one of two places! Close to home, like close enough for them to keep their eyes on the other party to ensure the safety of the secret or so far away from home that you'd never be able to find the guy. Meaning she met a man on vacation gave him some, snapped the pussy back, and brought it home to you as if nothing happened, and in her mind, shit, it didn't, lol.

An example of a woman who's TTG moment occurs close to home is when she sleeps with a male friend, a family member of her boyfriend or someone in her natural course of life like her boss or business partner. The reason being, she knows that if it were to come out, both parties would be in some deep shit, thus eliminating the risk of the guy running his mouth. Whereas when it occurs far away from home, she knows that at this point, it didn't happen, and with the lack of sufficient evidence of there being another party involved, it's all in your head created by your insecure imagination.

All TTG moments aren't a one-time thing. In fact, in most cases, they are full-blown sex affairs that last as long as nothing jeopardizes it. What could jeopardize it? Almost getting caught, and changing circumstances that eliminate the leverage over the third party like a man catching feelings or moving without care as if he doesn't mind being caught.

Do note that if a woman is truly on the verge of getting caught, she may come clean, but that won't happen until she's caught nearly red-handed or while in the act. Anything shy of that will just be an argument that she would most likely win due to insufficient evidence. Damn, women are so smart.

"A dangerous woman is one that can live with her emotions and not base her decisions off of them."

~ Wolf ~

See, understand this, and I mentioned it briefly in an earlier chapter, women cheat with a purpose, the extent of that purpose determines if the offense is Manslaughter or Capital, which is where intent would play a factor. A woman who commits woman slaughter knows what she wants out of the situation and doesn't take nor ask for anything additional. She can drop it and move on from it, living a completely normal and wholesome life without her man ever suspecting a thing.

Some women even have men unknowingly caring for children that aren't theirs. Not all women are expert cheaters though; there are women out here moving stupidly or as I like to call it recklessly. Those are the females that get caught, end up pregnant, with an STD, or in love with the other man. In rare cases, a female can't live with the guilt of her actions and end up telling on herself.

In any case, where something like that is to occur, it is capital behavior and no longer considered to be Manslaughter regardless of her confessing due to such malicious activity.

Chapter 6

Manslaughter vs. Capital: Understanding the Terms

If you have any understanding as to how the criminal justice system works, I think it's safe to say that you have an overall understanding of what is considered to be Manslaughter vs. what is considered to be capital murder.

Now, for all of my law students who may be reading this, I am aware that there are multiple levels to Manslaughter as well as different degrees to murder, keep in mind that I am merely making a comparison using an analogy! No one is actually on trial for murder here, Got it? Good! Back to the book.

If you have an understanding of the differences in Manslaughter vs. capital murder, you'll understand that any individual convicted of either offense will still be considered a murderer and serve time in prison. The amount of time served, or the punishment inflicted will vary based on the level of offense the suspect is charged with.

Now, my definition is similar in a variety of ways. I just prefer a different style of punishment that doesn't involve someone spending time away in prison. The similarities between my definition of manslaughter/capital and the description you may find in any law book or like, for my case, Google™, are synonymous with the surface of Capital being extremely more heinous than Manslaughter and deserving of a much more crucial punishment.

Capital is planned and committed with ill intent and Manslaughter; however, still, a severe offense is committed without malice. Now step away from your emotional mind for a second and eliminate all of the things you've personally experienced. Now, I ask that you step inside of your rational mind beyond your already established logistical way of thinking and follow along with me as I define the terms in depth. Keep an open mind as you read.

Manslaughter: is when a man/woman engages in any form of sexual activity in the spur of the moment without being in the right state of mind. Those states include but are not limited to Intoxication, Anger, Sadness, or Vulnerability. As humans, it is almost in our nature to make our decisions based on the emotional state of mind that we are in when it is time to make the decision. When happy, we make different decisions than we do when we are sad or angry; when intoxicated, we make different decisions than we would if we were sober.

Now, there's some irrational psychological yoga doing vegan living philosophical minded person out there that will argue up, down and around the corner that humans should have the ability to make the same decisions no matter what state the mind is in. I won't argue against that as a possibility for SOME humans, maybe like one percent. But the vast majority of humans are unable to live in such a disciplined state of mind.

The truth is, in most cases, our emotions shape our decisions and our ability to make them rationally. This is why there are different degrees to murder. Even in the eyes of the criminal justice system, a person in a particular state of mind shouldn't be held to the same level of accountability for their actions as a person considered to be in a "normal" state of mind. It should be viewed the same way regarding cheating. Manslaughter can be broken down into two parts, Involuntary and Voluntary; the determining factor on if a man/woman cheating is committing voluntary or involuntary can be assessed once you understand the difference between the two.

Involuntary Manslaughter: For example, a man at a party drinking approached by an attractive female who invites him into the bathroom to suck his dick, shouldn't be held to the same standard of a man who was soberly texting a female, invited her over while his girlfriend was at work, and got some head in their bed. Were both men wrong? Absolutely. But is party guy deserving of the same punishment as in the bed head dude? Nooooo.

There's a possibility that the party guy was accepting that invitation to the bathroom whether he was drunk or not, but there's no substantial proof that could conclude that. Therefore, he gets off with a slap on the wrist. Why is that? Because intoxication increases temptation and decreases rationality.

By now, you're asking yourself, "well, if a woman is at the same party and decides to allow a man to eat her pussy or she decides to suck his dick in the bathroom, is it considered the same?" Of course, fucking not!! Lol, I'm just kidding. Of course, it is. Although it is unlikely to happen, an intoxicated woman is awarded the same lead way as the drunk man, why? Because we are all human, and being intoxicated can affect us all in a way in which we cannot be held entirely accountable for our behavior.

Now nothing I'm saying here means that you can blame all of your infidelities on being intoxicated or that right before you go on a cheating spree, you can take a shot of liquor and blame it on the goose. Nor am I saying that you will be forgiven for cheating while intoxicated. I am saying it should be viewed differently in the eye of the public as well as your partner considering no harm was consciously intended when the decision was made. Still, of course, it's determined by the perspective of the person viewing it.

Voluntary Manslaughter: Caters to the other states of mind that fall under Manslaughter, which includes: Vulnerability, Sadness, and Anger. Mix all 3 of these emotions in one and guess what you get? SPITE!! And many women tend to act out of it when hit by all three emotions at once. We all have heard the term spite, and some of us have even found ourselves using it to describe the actions of our partners. The reason spite classifies as Manslaughter is because although it's a malicious act, it is performed passionately under uncontrollable emotional circumstances due to the initial actions of their partner, it's like a cause and effect thing. Without the initial action, there'd be no reaction, therefore, excusing the behavior of the spiteful woman. Women experience spite in phases starting with extreme sadness followed by intense anger topped off with enhanced vulnerability.

All of these emotions bottled up and released into a conversation with that "understanding" male friend makes for some good "I'm going to regret this tomorrow, but it feels good right now" sex. Now, for those of you who are wondering, "how can a woman who knows she's going to regret it tomorrow qualify for Manslaughter after going through with the action of having sex with another man?" It is because she is in no real rational state of mind when faced with making that decision, and she is searching for a way to release her hurt and feel whole again while also wanting her man to pay for his actions by hopefully causing him the same pain he caused her.

The crazy part about it is, a girl in this predicament wants her man to feel how she felt but wouldn't want him to find out. Instead, it'll just go down as a TTG moment for her, but she's okay with that because, ultimately, she just wants to release her pain and hurt without her man finding out. Even after cheating himself, if a man were ever to find out about his girlfriend cheating on him, he would consider her to be disloyal. Women don't live by a man's definition of loyalty, and they never will, so there's no point in trying to apply it to them. Men follow certain principles that women simply don't. Women see loyalty as don't do to me what you don't want me to do to you. Women are loyal to their emotions, and that's just that! If she's sad, angry, vulnerable, or all three, you can kiss that "loyalty" goodbye, it went out the window with her happiness, and spite has made an untimely arrival.

A man also can act out of spite under the same circumstances faced with those same emotions. A man that was cheated on is more likely to cheat out of spite than a woman. That's if he decides to stay with his girlfriend. Men will act out of spite after being cheated on because they too are searching for an emotional release and a way to feel whole again after being completely torn apart. A man's pride and ego eat away at him every time he envisions his woman in bed with another man. Depending on the strength of the man's ego, that will determine how often he is likely to cheat trying to convince himself that he's the man that any woman would die to have.

The difference in men and women acting out of spite is, a woman would want her man to feel what she felt but wouldn't want him to find out, as I stated before. Men, on the other hand, not only would want their woman to experience the same pain he's feeling, his ego would entice him to rub it in by moving recklessly in hopes of providing her with the same public humiliation he felt.

In either case, both men and women face embarrassment. Women are more than likely to elect to pass on the opportunity to publicly humiliate their spouse because they know it'll embarrass themselves as well. Man, you have to appreciate the maturity of a woman. By now, I think it's safe to say we have an understanding of what the act of Manslaughter is, now it's time for me to break down the action of Capital.

Capital Behavior: By far, the worst behavior to exhibit in a relationship. In most cases, there's no restoring the damages done to the relationship caused by such ill-advised activity.

Unlike with Manslaughter, where a lot of occurrences can be rectified with effective communication and understanding. Capital behavior is a lot tougher to come back from because the wounds created by it are so deep-rooted, it causes mental and emotional trauma that's long-lasting and requires time to heal.

Capital behavior, for example, would be a man dealing with his ex or baby mom or a woman dealing with her ex or baby father. This type of behavior is considered Capital because, as stated in an earlier chapter, it is bringing life back to what was supposed to be a situation that died long ago.

Most new relationships cross the bridge of exes, with the new partner needing to know if the chapter has concluded with the doors being closed all the way with no anger, guilt, or resentment still seeping through the cracks. If those emotions are still looming, it would indicate that the relationship isn't completely over, and any forward motion into a new relationship would be happening prematurely, which doesn't bode well for anyone. No one wants to be the rebound, and nobody wants to feel like you're settling for them.

So, when you set out to move on in your new relationship, any activity of reverting to your "ex" is considered capital behavior and is extremely difficult to recover from. Your new spouse will always carry insecurities and thoughts on if you're settling for them, if the previous relationship ever ended in the first place and if there are any emotions still attached to your past relationship.

Another example of capital behavior would be, baby mother or baby father dealings. These types of situations will terminate a relationship because although they carry the same insecurities and worries that stem from dealing with an ex, these situations have NO end because there's a child involved, which means there has to be communication between mommy and daddy. They have to be involved in each other's lives to be effectively co-parenting for the child.

Now what I am saying does not indicate that someone with a child is not someone you can have a long-lasting and successful relationship with. I'm saying that if the person you are dealing with isn't finished with their child's other parent, it won't work. Capital behavior will end up terminating the relationship.

Any situation involving an ex or a co-parent will create hurdles to face in the relationship, and the chances of the relationship surviving them are very slim to none.

I know some of these statements are going to raise the question on if any offenses fall in between Manslaughter and Capital, I will answer that question right here and right now. Yes! Some offenses are too severe to be considered Manslaughter, whether voluntary or involuntary, and not severe enough to be regarded as capital behavior.

In any case, where someone is cheating in between the confines of Manslaughter and Capital, they would fall in the grey area; this grey area constitutes the statue of **First-Degree** or **Second-Degree,** depending on the facts of the incident.

The difference between first-degree and second-degree is determined by how many acts of premeditation are included while committing the offense. There are 6 acts of premeditation in total, I've listed them and explained the terms.

The Six Acts of Premeditation: are any acts of cheating performed: Calculated, Purposefully, Recklessly, Deliberately, Intentionally, or Emotionally.

Calculation: The act of moving strategically.

Purposefully: The act of moving with a purpose, like in hopes of moving on, or filling a void of lack in the relationship.

Recklessly: Moving with no regard or no respect for the relationship, for example: carrying yourself like you are single.

Deliberately: To act spitefully in a deliberate manner with the intent of hurting your relationship.

Intentionally: The act of setting intentions while cheating, similarly, to moving with a purpose but more severe because instead of having hopes of moving on, one sets real plans on moving on.

Emotionally: The act of developing feelings while cheating and allowing those feelings to contribute to your decision-making process causing you to move emotionally, for example, falling in love, downplaying your relationship, and protecting the feelings of the person you're cheating with.

Now that we have an understanding of the six acts of premeditation, I can explain what constitutes second-degree and what constitutes first-degree.

Second-Degree: is the lesser of the two offenses, it is a step up from voluntary Manslaughter because it includes one act of premeditation. For instance, in the section about voluntary Manslaughter, I went on to explain the difference between women moving out of spite vs. men moving out of spite, remember?

Well, the male's actions can be described as a second-degree offense. To paraphrase: a man moving recklessly or deliberately out of spite is subjected to fall under the statue of second degree as opposed to voluntary Manslaughter because of his premeditated intent. Had this same man committed the same act out of spite without being deliberate or moving recklessly, he would fall under voluntary Manslaughter.

Women are way less likely to fall under the second-degree statue because, as explained above, women who are committing the act of voluntary Manslaughter do not include any of the six premeditated actions to raise their offense to second-degree. In the event where a woman that committed voluntary Manslaughter did include one of the six acts of premeditation, she too will be subjected to second-degree.

Only one act of premeditation has to be determined for a cheating offense to be raised from voluntary Manslaughter to second-degree. If two acts of premeditation are committed, the offense now would be crossing into the threshold of first-degree.

First-Degree: Is the middle-child between second-degree and Capital behavior because it is the very thin line that separates second-degree from capital behavior. It is one premeditated act away from either being a Capital offense or a Second-degree offense making it tricky to understand. In simple terms, first-degree is where two acts of premeditation are committed while voluntarily cheating.

The tricky part comes into play when you factor in which two of the six premeditated actions are involved. For example: moving deliberately OR recklessly constitutes second-degree, while moving deliberately AND recklessly is considered to be a first-degree offense because two acts of premeditation are involved.

For instance: a person cheating, whether it be male or female moving in a calculated and deliberate manner, would be considered to be a first-degree offense, swap out deliberate with intentionally, and you have yourself a capital offense. Why? Because the act of strategically moving with set intentions is a recipe for building a bridge from your current relationship to your new one.

Another example of first-degree would be acting recklessly in a deliberate manner. These kinds of scenarios tend to occur during that "break period" of a relationship that has run its course but hasn't finalized an ending agreement from both parties.

The reason deliberately moving with recklessness is considered first degree, as opposed to capital behavior, is because of one or two instances. There were no set intentions on moving on, no purpose nor calculation, and there were no emotions involved outside of sadness, anger, and vulnerability. Just a hurt man/woman that wants to inflict payback on their spouse for the humiliation and pain they've caused them after discovering they were cheated on.

The second scenario could be the break period providing both parties with a hall-pass to "Do You." One party decides to exercise that right, and the other one decides not to. This wouldn't even be an offense at all if the relationship were never to be mended.

First-degree can be summed up as any two acts of premeditation committed while cheating that doesn't involve setting intentions or moving emotionally. Any act of cheating that includes intentions or emotions is considered capital behavior no matter which of the other acts of premeditation they are paired with. A relationship cannot survive the turmoil caused by a man or woman moving emotionally, which includes downplaying their relationship to protect the feelings of the person they're cheating with or being in love with another person, this is why it constitutes as capital behavior.

There is also no returning from set intentions because once a man or woman sets plans to pursue a new relationship, their current relationship is over even if they decide to stay together. I think it's safe to say that cheating is painful to endure, no matter what offense was committed by your partner. Still, I stand firmly on the circumstances having a massive indication of if the relationship can be mended or not.

There are many occasions in which someone we know and love was cheated on and made the decision to stay with their cheating spouse to work things out. Some of us even made the statement "that could never be me" and ended up in that same situation we said we would never be in making the same decision we said we would never make. The reason being is because of the terms used and described in this chapter. Truth is these terms existed way before you and me. I just found a cool way to phrase them to help you and everyone else out there understand when it's okay to work through the problems in your relationship caused and created by cheating. Not to say that you have to work it out, nor is it to say that the person at fault can pull out this book like it's the constitution, refer to these terms and examples, and be instantly off the hook.

This chapter is to help people understand why they may have made the decision to stay and work things out or why they may make the decision in the future to do so. It is also to help us understand what goes into the decision-making process and not to judge each other for deciding to work things out.

Defining the Terms

Manslaughter: is when a man/woman engages in any form of sexual activity in the spur of the moment or while not in the right state of mind. Those states include but are not limited to Intoxication, Anger, Sadness, or Vulnerability.

Involuntary Manslaughter: is when a man or woman commits an act of cheating impulsively while intoxicated or in an irrational state of mind. It's a heat of the moment type of thing.

Voluntary Manslaughter: A rational decision made irrationally due to being in the vulnerable, sad, or angry state of mind.

Second Degree: Cheating voluntarily while including one act of premeditation. Excluding emotions or intentions.

First Degree: Cheating Voluntarily while including two acts of premeditation. Excluding emotions or intentions.

Capital Behavior: Any act of cheating committed involving emotions or intentions.

The Six Acts of Premeditation: Any act of cheating performed: Calculated, Purposefully, Recklessly, Deliberately, Intentionally, or Emotionally.

Chapter 7

Intent Changes Everything: Explaining My Points

Most women would say that I am biased or that I'm inevitably more on the side of men because I am a man. Would I agree with them? No, but I cannot deny the fact that I am a man. I'm not going to allow my opinion to be discredited, belittled, or diluted from the perspective of women who fail to be openminded to a man having an understanding of the tendencies of women.

If this were a matter of abortion, pregnancy, childbirth, or a female's menstrual cycle, I would agree with that. As a man, no matter how much I try to understand it, that's just not something we men can understand because it's not something we've experienced. We can empathize and show compassion, but the reality is, it's not an area where we as men can truly form an opinion. I stay away from those topics with my male point of view. I've learned through my experiences that women rarely respect the opinion of a man on matters regarding women. I've also learned that women want men to show compassion and empathy but don't want men to develop an opinion on them or subjects, circumstances, and matters that pertain to them.

Although, women feel they can develop an opinion on men even if the opinion they've formed is bias, stereotypical, or just flat out wrong. Cheating is something both men and women experience and are affected by. Who are we to assume that one gender is affected differently than the other? Where's the empathy in that?

I would never say that cheating affects men any differently than it affects women, and I would never say that a man and woman should be viewed any differently for committing the same act of cheating.

What I will say is what I've been saying throughout this entire book, cheating cannot be generalized as to say "cheating is cheating" because it is a case by case situation. The views of it are circumstantial contingent upon the details involved. Everything changes behind intent always have and always will, that's transparent in all aspects of life.

If you're a basketball player and decide to foul another player in an aggressive manner with the intent of hurting or injuring that player, it is called a flagrant foul; in football, it's called a personal foul or unnecessary roughness. In boxing, it's referred to as a low blow or unlawful blow. These offenses can result in ejection, disqualification, a fine and, in some cases, a suspension because there was intent to hurt another player, and the referee's job is to keep sports fair but, more importantly, safe.

Intent changes everything in your everyday life as well. See, it like this, you're walking down the street, and another person walks past and bumps you, depending on how you perceive the intent behind this person bumping you is what will determine your reaction.

If you are walking down a sidewalk filled with people with little room for anyone to maneuver, you'd most likely view it as unintentional and proceed with your day. Now, if the sidewalk was empty and this individual was to bump into you, you'd more than likely view it as intentional and issue a completely different response than you would if the circumstances had been as I first described.

See? When we view someone's actions to be intentional, we consider the situation in a completely different light as opposed to something we view as unintentional. Intent doesn't change the facts of what happened; in both cases, you were indeed bumped, but intent changes your views on being bumped.

Truth is we've all experienced hurt unintentionally before, whether it was from someone with an opinion that we valued telling us they don't like our outfit or from our parents making life decisions for our lives without our consent. Did we punish our loved ones in our mind for these things? Yes! But we've let it go over time. Had we perceived the actions of our loved ones to be with the intent to hurt us, the pain would be much more crucial to us and even harder to get over.

If we can successfully develop an understanding of why intent is so important when viewing the actions of another human being, we'd be able to rationalize our responses, whether they be emotional, mental, or verbal.

I described a woman's act of cheating to be capital behavior because of what goes into the decision-making process of most women that elect to cheat. I described a man's act of cheating to be manslaughter on the surface but also went on to explain when a man's actions should be considered capital behavior based on intent.

Look at it this way; a man is way more likely to cheat than a woman is, a man is also more than likely to cheat with multiple partners. A man will cheat for the sole purpose of boosting his ego. 90% of the time, a man will sleep with women just to be able to say to himself "I'm the man" and every woman he's able to sleep with only further entices that thought.

Women aren't out here sleeping with men just to say to themselves, "I'm that girl" because it doesn't boost their ego, if anything it does the opposite, it makes them feel less of themselves even if it feels right at the moment. Women have insecurities about themselves that make them self-conscious; they wouldn't reveal those insecurities to a man until they are comfortable. Women would much rather get it right the "first time" to avoid having to open up mentally, physically, and emotionally to multiple men.

Men, in more cases than not, don't cheat from an emotional standpoint, and because a man doesn't have to develop emotions to cheat, it's easier for him to decide to cheat. It's more impulse than anything. The world is full of temptation for both men and women. Still, the time it takes to develop an emotional connection for someone limits the number of people they will cheat with because we as humans cannot connect emotionally with everyone.

Cheating with emotions changes everything. It adds intent, and purpose, which then leads to calculated actions, whether they be reckless and deliberate or not. If you don't believe my theory by now, ask a woman what sex means to her, she'll respond along the lines of sex being sacred, ask a man what sex means to him he'll tell you it depends on his partner.

Women need to understand; men are not emotionally opening up for any and every woman by allowing them to see his soft side. Now, here's an area where both men and women are similar: women nor men will open up to just anybody. The only difference is, a man doesn't open his heart or his legs to have sex; this is the reason why men view sex differently than women.

Saying this doesn't indicate that women develop feelings for every man they sleep with, or that they are incapable of cheating the same amount or even more than a man because, in some cases, there are women out there who move, act and think like men.

What does it consist of to "think like a man" to my definition? Making emotionless decisions to satisfy temporary temptations that fulfill temporary needs with no regard for any future consequences.

Are those women any more wrong than the men who do the same thing? Heck no! Does society see it differently? Of course, they do! Is this ok and appropriate to view it differently? Heck no! But we cannot ignore the fact that there's a double standard that exists in society.

I'm not sure if it's possible to eliminate the men vs. women cheating double standard that exist because it's so deep-rooted and comprised of many other double standards that exist between men and women. I will go more in-depth about the double standard in the chapter to follow.

For now, we must understand how much of a factor intent play into how we view the actions of another human being. Having an understanding won't eliminate the cheating double standard. Still, it could help us to limit it if everyone starts to view a man and woman's actions to be equally deserving of the same punishment based on the intent behind their actions.

Chapter 8

Stop Ignoring the Double Standard

How long will we as a people continue to ignore the existence of double standards? I mean, they are a part of our everyday life for crying out loud. Double standards are what shaped and created the norms, stigmas, stereotypes, perceptions, and even the "morals" that existed then and still exist in our society to this very day, stemming far beyond cheating.

Double standard, by definition, states a rule or principle which applies unfairly in different ways to different people or groups. So, in other words, a double standard is society saying it's ok for one person or group of people to do something, but it's not ok for another person or group of people to do the same thing.

Is this a problem? Yes, it is! But ignoring and suppressing a problem doesn't make it go away, not even for a moment. The real problem with double standards isn't their existence. The problem is people in society picking and choosing which double standards they honor and which ones they want to banish. If we're going to eliminate double standards as a whole, the real work starts from within. That's correct; we as individuals have to correct the things within us that create the mental contradiction that says one double standard is ok, and others are absurd.

I don't agree that one double standard should be acceptable, and another shouldn't. I mean, isn't that a double standard in itself? I feel that you can't be partially against something, you're either all out, or you are all in by default. There is no in-between. See, I always believed that to eliminate a problem, you have to address it head-on and get to the source of the problem. You stop a problem in its root, always has, and always will. In this particular case, double standards are deeply rooted in all of us, with race, age, gender, ethnicity, religion, sexuality, military, crime, and economic class.

I mean, we see and hear these things all the time. It's ok for adults to use curse words but not ok for a child. A man providing for a woman is expected while a woman providing for a man makes the man weak. It's ok to judge people who have different religious beliefs than you. Murder is ok if you're in the army but illegal for regular US citizens. If a doctor sells it to you its medicine, if you buy it from the guy on the corner, it's drugs. I can go on and on about all of the everyday instances where double standards play a factor. That is just a few, to say the least. Life is saturated with double standards.

Life is a series of events compiled together where humans judge other humans as to what's appropriate or inappropriate based on their views on the subject at hand. If you've found yourself partaking in any of it, then guess what? You, too, are a part of the problem. What I will say is, although double standards shape our beliefs, we didn't choose them, they were instilled into us throughout our upbringing. All we heard was, boys have to display strength while girls are allowed to cry if they're upset, girls have to respect their bodies by watching how they dress while boys don't have to, that is not ladylike, or that is not manly.

For our entire lives, we were all being programmed to view men and women differently. With that being said, perspectives and judgments change depending on if it's a man or woman. If a man hits a woman, he's more likely to receive ridicule than if a woman hits a man because it is proclaimed that a man is stronger than a woman, which isn't always necessarily true. A man sleeping with 20 women is cool, while a woman sleeping with 20 men makes her a slut.

So, there's undoubtedly a double standard with men and women, but we can't decide to raise the issue only when it applies to us personally. If you're against double standards, you have to deem all forms of double standards inappropriate, and it is not until you're able to do so that there will be noticeable changes in society. The problem starts and ends with us. It'll take the will power of every human being equally pushing for a difference to create change to this matter in particular.

The issue with that is, most people try to solve internal problems externally. Everyone is always looking to point the finger, looking for someone or something else to blame, taking no accountability for the role they contribute to enhancing the problem.

Look at it like this, let's compare humans with a tainted perspective to a car with a faulty engine or transmission. It doesn't matter how beautiful the car is on the outside, it will not function properly because the real work needs to be done under the hood. The same goes for humans preaching healing and advocating for change with a tainted, judgmental, or bias perspective. We can't change anything outside of ourselves.

As long as we start and continue to work on improving ourselves, we are contributing to the solution and not the problem, thus eliminating the problem. If you want double standards to go away, remove them from your ways of thinking.

Chapter 9

Pride and Ego

The biggest misconception that exists today regarding relationships is that cheating is what causes breakups, but it's not cheating that causes the breakup! It's pride and ego.

See, truth be told; most people are unaware of the significance in the roles played by pride and ego in a relationship. People often neglect how big of an influence both have on your ability to rationalize your decisions because most people don't know how to identify pride and ego within themselves. The ego will make you do something that your partner's pride cannot accept. It's like a cause and effect type of thing, ego being the cause and pride being the effect, and in some cases, the other way around.

Ego in one person will always trigger the pride in another person, and the pride in one person will always trigger the ego in another person. Pride and ego exist in all of us, but the two cannot coexist in a relationship between two people. Whether you're a man or a woman, the strength of pride and ego's existence in each of us individually will forever be the biggest weakness in all relationships.

With that being said, if you want your relationship to last, your ego must be tamed, and your pride must be intact. The difference between ego and pride is, ego has to be fed and satisfied externally while pride; on the other hand, is satisfied internally. Pride is that little voice in your head that appears when you feel taken advantage of that makes you stand up for yourself. It's that voice in your head that makes you say to yourself, "I refuse to put up with this." Ego is the voice that appears in your head that makes you say to yourself, "they got me f*cked up," which will be triggered when there is a lack of being respected, valued, praised and validated by others.

See, pride is what you think, know, and feel about yourself, while ego is what others think, know, and feel about you. If either of these voices gets too loud in your head, they will gain strength and begin to control your mind. Now, I know most of you who are reading this is thinking to yourself that pride must be more appropriate to have than ego if pride is the part of you protecting and standing up for yourself, but that's not always the case. Yes! The presence of pride is set up in all of us as something to be proud and appreciative of because having our pride is a way to measure our integrity and dignity to know when things go against our morals. Making it ok to take pride in who you are as a person and what you stand for because this gives us our sense of integrity, which gives us a reason to be prideful.

For those reasons, the presence of pride is indeed helpful and appropriate, since it assists us in knowing when to draw the line that goes against our moral compass. The problem arises with pride when it has no boundaries on how thick that line should be when it comes to protecting ourselves from the things that go against our moral compass. Which then leads to having too much pride. See, pride isn't a threat to you until it becomes too strong. Once that happens, it will amplify even the smallest of problems by making you think it goes against your moral compass.

There's only one way to weaken your pride, and that is by understanding your moral compass. Your moral compass is comprised of the things that direct your spirit. When you're doing something within the perimeters of your moral compass, you'll know because it feels natural and familiar, so your spirit is unbothered and doesn't feel the need to protect itself. When you're doing something outside of your moral compass, your spirit is affected and uncomfortable because it is not natural to be treading unfamiliar territory. Unfamiliar territory is anything that goes directly against your moral compass.

For example, a woman who views sex as sacred wouldn't feel morally right to have a meaningless one-night stand because it goes against her moral compass, which would be considered an unfamiliar territory. Unfamiliar territory activates the need for protection of your spirit, thus activating your pride to redirect your moral compass by telling it to thicken that line of integrity and dignity.

Thickening your integrity and dignity creates the presence of a strengthened pride if done as a protection mechanism. A strengthened pride will confuse your moral compass because your moral compass operates through spirit, while pride operates through the mind.

Look at it like this; let's say that woman I referred to earlier was to have sex on the first night with a man she liked and then, later on, regret it because she never received a callback. Her moral compass will activate her pride because it would resemble much of a meaningless one-night stand; this would then affect her ability to rationalize the situation. The only thing she would consider is that she went against her moral compass by having sex on the first night. Once she arrives at that conclusion, she is likely never to have sex on the first night again. Her pride will instill it into her mind that sex on the first night is wrong and that it goes against her moral compass when, in reality, time isn't even a key component to your moral compass. It doesn't matter if you sleep with someone on the first day or the 100th day, the fact is that not everyone who you have sex with views it as sacred and you will never know what their views are until after you have sex with them, making the woman's conclusion wrong. Time is not the reason for her disappointment, and she never actually went against her moral compass.

The outcome resembling the one-night-stand, which does go against her moral compass, is what activated her pride and created that confusion. If her pride wasn't activated, she would realize that it wasn't the amount of time that created her disappointment and accept the fact that she felt she was making the right decision at that moment. Even though the outcome wasn't the one she wanted. Doing so would allow her to realign with her moral compass and operate out of rationality moving forward as opposed to avoiding those types of situations in totality due to the fear of getting an outcome she doesn't want. Once your pride is strengthened, your ability to react rationally is weakened.

Too much pride confuses the moral compass because the boundaries it once knew are no longer, and the new boundaries have no limit to how far it will extend to protect you. Too much pride hurts more than it helps because it blocks as many good experiences as it does the bad ones. A strengthened pride has to control the outcome of every situation, and when it's unable to control the outcome, it creates confusion in your mind causing a blockage that stops you from doing whatever you want to do. Pride can paralyze you from making a decision by putting your mind against your spirit, making it nearly impossible to know what decision is right for you.

Pride has the advantage over the moral compass because it reacts faster than the moral compass, or at least we perceive it that way. The real truth is, spirit always appears first, but pride can make you question if what you're feeling in spirit is correct or if your mind is playing tricks on you, and since pride operates inside the mind, it can take control over it. Making it essential to understand your moral compass and how it operates so you can operate inside of it to avoid activating your pride.

The best way to understand your moral compass is by knowing what your morals are. You have to know what you are comfortable with and what you're not comfortable with before pride taints your perspective. Knowing your morals and living by them will keep pride intact because you won't find yourself treading unfamiliar territory. You'll also know when you or someone else is doing something that goes against your moral compass, giving you the ability to handle the situation rationally and without pride. We consider this to be putting our pride aside. After understanding pride and what it does to the spirit, you have to understand ego and what it does to your identity.

I'll start by saying this, to tame your ego, you must first understand what ego is, how it develops, what triggers it, and then how to tame it. Ego is one of the biggest most misunderstood elements of someone's character. Look at it like this; for most people, when they think about ego, they instantly affiliate it with being boastful, cocky, arrogant, and full of yourself. Although true to some degree, those characteristics are a result of an ego that has already developed. They are not a part of the ego's developmental process. The height of your self-esteem determines the strength of your ego, if you have high self-esteem, you'll have a strong ego, but if you have low self-esteem, you're most definitely subjected to having a weak ego. Weak egos constantly crave attention and satisfaction. The reason self-esteem is a huge indication of how strong or weak of an ego you have is because a weak ego has to be stroked externally by the opinions and validity of others to be satisfied.

You tend to see people with low self-esteem trying to keep up with the latest trends to be socially accepted. Whereas high self-esteem generates self-confidence, which is internal, which results in self-validation, so there's no need to do things to fit in because you're already comfortable with yourself. A good way to measure your ego is by knowing how and if you compare yourself to others. Comparison is the thief of joy because it creates jealousy, envy, greed, and the need to be first, which is typically found in someone with a weak ego. A person with a strong ego has no desire to compete nor compare themselves to anyone because the confidence they have makes them comfortable with themselves and their position in the world. Someone with a strong ego doesn't find joy in tearing others down to feel first because they don't view life as a competition between them and other people.

If your self-confidence is high, you'll have a sense of self-identity, and you'll know what's for you and what's not for you, leaving no room for a weak ego to operate. Weak ego lacks identity, which means the ego doesn't know itself. So, in other words, your ego has to constantly be attached to something to be given life because weak egos cannot survive on their own. Consider a weak ego to be homeless when it's without identity. What gives that weak ego a place to call home and an identity? YOU. That's correct; you give the weak ego an identity by not knowing yourself. When you don't know yourself, you create a vacancy within you that a homeless ego cannot wait to fill.

Understand this, allowing the weak ego in is a choice, but it's not a choice we make with the consciousness of what it does to our self-identity. The identity we give to our weak ego is an illusion that we are giving an identity to ourselves. We think we are doing a service to ourselves when in actuality, it's a disservice because this weak ego takes us further away from who we truly are and our sense of self. Once the weak ego detaches us from our sense of self, it creates low self-esteem, which, as a result, makes us feel empty or unsure of ourselves. No one likes the feeling of feeling empty or unsure of themselves because it gives life to insecurities. Since our ego can silence insecurities by providing assurance temporarily, we feed it. The issue with that assurance provided by the weak ego is that it's false assurance because it doesn't come directly from us. It comes from things outside of us, like the praise and positive opinions of others; this means it's not truly ours. So, it can be easily taken away from us once the praise is gone, and the positive opinions are no longer feeding our ego.

The validation, opinions, and praise of others are like pain medicine for the weak ego. It solves your problem temporarily, but after a while, the feeling fades, and the pain returns, thus creating a higher tolerance and the constant need for more. Real assurance cannot be tampered with and can only be provided by one's self through self-validation, not through validation provided by things that feed the weak ego.

Don't get me wrong; it's ok to appreciate the positive opinions and praise of others, but you must not allow it to become the base of your identity, subjecting you to it becoming a necessity for you to feel valued in the world. Having a weak ego is like having a job in which you can be fired at any time because the only position it holds is the one provided by others. So, there's no real security in it, and you'll constantly live in fear of losing it. Self-confidence is like being an entrepreneur. No one can take from you what they didn't give to you! It is the efforts of your mindset that determine your results.

So, in totality, having too much pride and a weak ego are equally detrimental to you and your relationships. Why? Because the presence of too much pride and a weak ego take a toll on your reasoning mind and tamper with your ability to make rational decisions. Too much pride and a weak ego will entice you to make irrational decisions 100% of the time. A weak ego in a man will create problems that a strengthened pride in a woman can hold on to, in most cases, longer than necessary.

Many people have no problem with saying they have too much pride without realization of the effects having too much pride can have on them. Having too much pride works against you because you'll refrain yourself from letting go of something so long to a point where you're only affecting yourself. Pride will convince you that walking away from a situation is the only solution even if at heart you want to stay.

Pride wasn't instilled in us for us to use as punishment to ourselves or others. Pride is supposed to help us navigate our moral compass with dignity and integrity. Instead, it has become the base of unforgiveness, creating the inability to move past a hurtful situation, because it eliminates our ability to be understanding.

You'll know if your pride or ego is triggered by way of how you act or react to a situation. Ego normally is an action that makes you feel good momentarily by receiving praise and validation, pride, on the other hand, is a reaction generated from feeling the need to protect yourself.

To summarize, pride wants things to be mutual, whereas ego wants all of the attention, praise, and validation. The ego will tell you that someone has to text you first every time, and because of who you are, they should be happy to have the privilege of texting you. Pride will tell you that you shouldn't have to text a person first every time because if that person wanted to talk to you, they'd hit you up first to show their mutual interest, even if you really want to talk to that person. Too much pride or a weak ego will sink any relationship, so knowing how to identify the two is imperative if you want to keep them at bay.

Chapter 10

His Weak Ego Made Him Do It; Her Strong Pride Couldn't Let It Go.

I took the last chapter as an opportunity to make sure that there was a clear and concise understanding of how to identify pride and ego within ourselves before being able to identify them in our relationships. A man's ego is more likely to get him into trouble than a woman's ego. A woman's pride is stronger than a man's pride, and the strength of that pride shows up more frequently for her than it does for him.

Relationships wouldn't go through so much turmoil if his ego weren't so weak, and her pride wasn't so strong. See, the truth is a man's ego, and a woman's pride brings more relationships to an end than cheating ever could. Still, there's this big misconception that cheating is the leading cause of a relationship coming to an end.

See, cheating is just the headline to the story in which many people fail to read from start to finish, but if you look into the details of what occurred, I can almost guarantee you that his weak ego made him do it and her strong pride couldn't let it go. Understand this, there's no gender role assigned to pride and ego, but through the nature of a man and the nature of a woman, it is almost fact that a man's ego is weaker than a woman's ego and a woman's pride is stronger than a man's pride. If you want a relationship with less confusion and more understanding, women need to understand the nature of a man's pride and ego, and men need to understand the nature of a woman's pride and ego.

A man's ego is what gives him his status in the world. It tells him where he ranks amongst other men. Men are constantly doing things to improve their rank. They buy nice clothes, flashy cars and expensive houses all as an attempt to improve their rank and stroke their ego. With the world changing daily, so does a man's rank, which is why men have to continue doing things to maintain their status.

Since no man wants to be considered a has-been or a slouch, men have to do things constantly to establish their position in the world. How a man is viewed through the eyes of the world matters to him. Those views aren't limited to just how women view men, but how they're viewed by the entire world. Even if women were not around, men would still want to have a high status or high ranking amongst the other men because although men desire to be admired by women, they still want to be respected by other men. This wouldn't matter if it were in men's sports, an all-boy camp or a prison! Men would still want to have a high status. It's in a man's nature to want to be viewed as "The Man," whether that be in the household, in his line of work, or just amongst his friends.

Men possess a competitive nature; it's been that way since the beginning of time, which makes it very common for a man to want his ego stroked in some way, shape, form, or fashion. To be number one for a man isn't something that is limited to just financial wealth, because money isn't the only thing that gives a man his status. If money didn't exist, there'd still have to be a way to measure a man's status. Men measure their status by what's in front of them and their desire to be the best at it, with that being said, if it was a competition on who could run the fastest, throw the furthest or be the strongest, you'd see each and every man doing their best to try to be the best at it.

This competition will take place no matter if women are present or not, but having women present amplifies a man's desire to be first. Men want the best cars, the most money, the most attractive women attracted to them and to be the most powerful. Even with a desire to have all of those things, men still understand that life isn't a fairytale, and you can't always get everything you want.

A man will know that he's not the richest, most handsome, most charming person in the world, so it wouldn't be hard for a man to accept that as fact. Men know that they aren't first in the whole entire world, they just want to be first in their world, however large that realm is. This is why men will settle for being first or the best at something, whatever that one thing is. I said all that to say, having multiple women, like with anything else to a man, is for his ranking, and having sex with them is for sport.

Men don't date multiple women as an attempt to fill the void of what they lack; a man already knows what he lacks and accepts it for what it is. Remember, it's not in a man's nature to have everything just to be first at something. Understanding the nature of a man's ego would eliminate the additional hurt and pain that women put themselves through, trying to identify what they lacked that made their man cheat. That's an answer most men can never provide for a woman because she has to realize that, men don't cheat due to lack of what their woman is missing, women cheat for lack of what their man is missing. A woman isn't going to cheat with a man for his money if her man has money. She's going to cheat with the man who gives her whatever her man isn't giving her. Like time, attention, and things like that.

With that being the primary reason why women cheat, they assume that it's the same for men. I assure you that a man does not measure the women he cheats with to his woman, that'll require too much thought, time, and effort. Not only that, but he also has no intention of replacing his woman with another woman. A man can have a woman with a big butt, he's still going to cheat with a woman that has a big butt, and if his woman's butt is small, he's not seeking women with big butts as a way to replace his woman.

If you keep a man fed and satisfied sexually, he'll never leave you, but that won't stop him from stepping out from time to time just to stroke his ego. Sex with another woman is for his ego, just to feel like he's still "got it," and there's nothing that can stop a man from wanting to test that out every now and then unless it's just not something that he cares for anymore. A man appreciates a good homecooked meal but will still stop at Wendy's every now and then to satisfy a temporary urge.

It's never to say that Wendy's is better than the meal he has at home. In fact, he knows and understands that it's not, which is why he'd never compare the two. Men aren't even looking for Wendy's to be better than their homecooked meal. Sometimes Wendy's is just convenient in that moment of need. This is the same logic that applies to a man that steps out to have sex with another woman.

A woman would have to leave her man unsatisfied completely over a long course of time before he starts to even think about leaving her for another woman. With it being in a woman's nature to nurture, love, and please and a man's nature to protect, provide, and be nurtured, men expect certain things from their woman as a requirement. All a woman has to do is meet those minimum requirements for her relationship to never be in jeopardy. The biggest mistake made by women is them thinking they have to meet each and every need of their man as a way to prevent him from cheating. This is how they end up drained and feeling under-appreciated.

Men don't expect their woman to fill every void just want them to cover the main areas of focus. Keep the energy good, make sure things are in order at home, and keep him fed and satisfied sexually. A man is not coming home if it doesn't feel like home to him. He's going to stay wherever it feels like home for him. It'll be more demoralizing for a woman to operate outside of her nature of pleasing her man. That is the only time a woman's relationship is in jeopardy by the presence of another woman. If a woman is making her man's life hard by tampering with his peace of mind, not satisfying him sexually, and not making sure he is well-fed, he's going to find a woman that'll make his life easy. By then, you'll see a dip in his presence, or you'll see him taking steps toward moving on, which would then become capital behavior.

A man that is having his needs met at home will always come home no matter how many times he steps out, but a man who isn't having his needs met at home is gone just like the effort he's no longer seeing from his woman. For the sake of his ego, if women understood the importance it served a man to be number one, she'd understand why he wants to be the head of the household, the only man she has eyes for, and the man she admires most. This comes naturally to a woman because it's in her nature to not care about pleasing any other man but her own. Nothing is more damaging to a man's ego than to feel as though his woman views another man to be more admirable than him, even with him understanding the possibilities of that, it still would be crushing for him to know.

A woman's ego is stronger than a man's ego because she doesn't require the validity of the outside world when it comes to a relationship, it's more about what her man thinks about her than it is about what other men think. The opinion, praise, or validation of a man other than her own holds no real merit to her. Although she'll appreciate the compliments from them, one million compliments from other men won't equal up to one compliment from her man.

With women, it's not about how many compliments they receive. It's about who the compliments are coming from. If those compliments are coming from everybody but her man, they're worthless. Those compliments are worthless because women know that when all is said and done, they're just words, and having a million men attracted to them doesn't bring them closer to marriage.

That's why women don't understand when their man gets jealous of the attention they receive from other men. The only attention that matters to them is the attention from their man. It's in a woman's nature to please her man, so she'll always do the things that he likes, and it doesn't bother her to do these things because naturally, it's in a woman's nature. Men assume that a woman keeping herself together and getting dolled up is to attract other men when it's actually to look good for him. All she wants is to be appreciated for getting dressed up and receive respect for the process she had to go through, just to hear her man say, "you look beautiful." Men see this as an attempt to appeal to other men, and they end up acting insecurely. This makes it difficult for a woman because instead of getting a compliment, she got a headache from an argument, and the worst part of all is he'll wonder why she never gets dressed up for him, not realizing that it's to avoid the arguments and headaches.

Men need to understand that It's easier for a woman to live outside of her ego. Women focus more on what they're feeling inside than what's going on outside. I mean, sure women would love to have the finest things, make the most money and be the prettiest one out the bunch, but when it's all said and done, that's not what provides them their true happiness. A woman's true happiness comes from inside, and if she's not feeling good or happy within, those things that provide "status" wouldn't matter.

I mean, we see it all the time, a woman starts dealing with a man for the things he can do for her financially and still end up feeling empty inside because he can't provide her the things that ultimately matter the most. Whether it be time and attention, or love and affection. With that being said, in more times than not, you see this same woman miserable, unhappy, walking away from the relationship or cheating.

Society has created an illusion that women need to be bought to be impressed. When in all reality, they're impressed by genuine effort to show how important they are to you and how much they're truly appreciated and valued, which can't be found in a gift.

I mean, don't get me wrong, sure women love gifts, but even a man spoiling a woman with gifts won't matter if the gifts aren't thoughtful. See, men spend time and money focusing on the gift when the true value for women is in the thought. It's the thought that counts! You hear it all the time. Women care about having the best man, not the most men. As long as you spare a woman from public humiliation and embarrassment, a woman's ego is silenced the majority of the time.

However, even when triggered from time to time, it's easy for her to tame it because things that hold surface value lose value over time, whether that be praise and attention from others or expensive gifts. Just as it is important for a woman to understand a man's ego, it is equally important for a man to understand a woman's ego. Women feel no need to maintain their personal status in the world because they're objective is to find unity with their partner.

The only status a woman worries about is the status of her relationship and the status of her man. It's not to say that women don't care about status at all; women just care about it for a different reason. Remember, women don't want the most men, they want the best man, and they know that a man with a high status gives them all the status they need. No woman wants a man that lacks respect, attention, and admiration from others, and men know that which further entices their desire to raise and maintain their status.

It's actually set up perfectly that a woman doesn't care for her own personal status because men don't prefer their woman to have status. If anything, men would rather avoid a woman with status because he'd have a fear of her ego being equivalent to his, craving the need to be stroked. Which will make a man run for cover.

Men have a possessive nature to want to protect what's theirs and wouldn't want other men to want their woman or worst; they wouldn't want for all the attention from other men to go to their woman's head. Men are ok with a man finding their woman attractive, but they want that interest to stop there. Women assume that a man fearing a woman with status is a result of her being a threat to him, financially or in authority, but that's not the case at all.

A man can find comfort in his woman making more money than him, as well as in splitting the decisions with her as long as she allows him to feel like he's the head of the household. A man can't find comfort in his woman attracting other men at large volumes if it appears to be going to her head because a man doesn't like to feel threatened in his position as the number one man in his woman's life.

This is why men prefer their women to be inaccessible to other men. A woman doesn't mind making herself inaccessible to other men if she feels the security of her position from her man. A woman not craving validation from other women or men for personal status is why her ego would never drive her to cheat. It wouldn't make a woman feel good to know she had sex with 30 men. If anything, it'll make her feel bad, like something is wrong with her. Even if a woman is a downright sex addict, she'd still prefer it to be with a man she loves and not just for the sake of doing it. A woman's views on stepping out of her relationship will always include something that's lacking in her relationship. She'd see no other valid justifiable reason to cheat if it's not adding an element to her life that's missing. To understand that women cheat to fill the void of what their relationship lacks while men cheat for the sport to maintain their status and boost their ego is to understand why his ego made him cheat and hers didn't.

Women and men that understand each other's ego tend to have a good understanding of one another. Still, for a relationship to survive the test of time, men and women would also have to have an understanding of each other's pride in the relationship. Luckily for humanity, a man's pride is nonexistent in a relationship until his pride is triggered.

A man's pride being triggered doesn't happen that often and even if it does, it doesn't last long because it's easy for a man to put his pride aside for his woman. Men have a strong pride only in instances where their ego is challenged or damaged.

For instance, a man's ego is challenged when he feels incapable of doing the things he's supposed to be doing as a man, like hold down his household responsibilities and fulfill his duties as the man of the

138

house. Even when things are spiraling out of control, a man's pride would be too strong to ask for help. Asking for help is a challenge to a man's ego because it lowers his status as a man if he's not able to handle his manly duties. We hear it all the time, a man who cannot handle his responsibilities as a man is not a man! A man's pride grows strong to protect himself from looking weak. So, a man may refrain from asking for directions if he's lost, help with carrying something heavy or assistance financially if he's struggling, just to avoid looking like he's incapable of fulfilling his duties as a man.

Men are taught growing up to follow God and the leadership of the man of their household. Until the time comes along for them to be the man of their own household.

This is why all men want to be leaders, and they want to appear like they have the solutions, especially in their household, because this is what men were taught. Men are supposed to lead, protect, and provide for their families. Doing anything that challenges that is going to challenge a man's ego and trigger a man's pride. It takes a certain level of humility in a man to be led by another man.

Truth be told, men only have pride in the presence of other men or when it involves other men. Men don't have any problem putting their pride aside for their women. When wrong, a man is never too proud to beg, say please or say sorry to his woman. Why? Because men were taught to take accountability for their actions, and men don't view an apology to their woman as looking or being weak. A man's ego isn't under attack in a situation involving him and his woman, and he understands the importance of the role she plays in his happiness as well as in keeping their house a home. We've all heard it before; if she's happy, then he's happy, which is why taking the initiative to make things right with her is never hard for him. Women have the power to silence a man's ego naturally by tapping into his emotions and activating his nurturing side or "soft side," as it is mostly referred to.

Not all women can activate this side of a man; only the woman he loves and considers to be his woman. Men are taught to be strong, which suppresses their emotions to refrain from being vulnerable and appearing weak. That is a mask that men wear to defend themselves from the attack of the world. Women have the power to remove that mask and open men up to releasing their emotions beyond their fears of vulnerability. With this being a power only possessed by a woman a man loves, a woman must understand how to harness that power without destroying the relationship.

Remember this, challenging a man's ego will never end the relationship, no matter how triggered a man's pride is, but once his ego is damaged, so is the relationship. Men can overcome the challenges that trigger their pride, but they cannot overcome the damages to their ego that trigger their pride. There's only one person with the power to damage a man's ego and guess who that person is? That's right! His woman and whether consciously or subconsciously, women know this.

Some women use this knowledge for understanding, and others use it for leverage, but I will say this to all women out there! Be careful with what you do with that information. You damage a man's ego, and you damage the man for good. There is nothing more damaging to a man's ego than to feel as though his woman finds another man to be more, admirable, attractive, or superior than him. Men know this to be a possibility, but the damage is done when it becomes a reality.

Men know very well what it takes to get the attention of a woman and, even more so, what it took to get the attention of his woman. Once another man has the attention of his woman, she's good as gone, and there's nothing left to fight for, with that being said, he can never forgive it. His pride will not allow him to because his ego is damaged. A man's ego is all he has in the world. It's his entire reputation, something he's been building since he was a child, so the woman he decides to be in a relationship with he's trusting her to guard and protect that reputation as if it were her own. The way a woman can protect her man's reputation is by not allowing another man the opportunity to be for her what her man can be, or worst, what her man cannot be. This is often referred to as giving "one-up" on them.

Men know that women aren't cheating for sport, even if they aren't able to express it verbally, they know and understand that a woman isn't giving her attention to a man that she isn't interested in, especially while a woman is in a relationship. Men also know that a woman is cheating to fill that void of lack, which is why men view women who cheat on them, as her giving another man one-up on him. To make matters worse, men understand that other men view it as gaining one up as well. That's correct! Men who sleep with another man's woman view it as an opportunity to gain one-up.

Men have no real intentions on moving on with a woman that's cheating on her man for him, reason being; all men understand the male code and how detrimental it is for a woman to give another man her attention while she's in a relationship. Even if he were to move on with her, he's bound to have a boatload of insecurities and fears of the same thing happening to him.

So, while a woman is cheating to fill a void of what her current relationship is lacking in hopes of moving on, the man she's cheating with isn't seeing it for anything other than what it is, an experience. Remember that men cheat for sport, whether they're being cheated with or doing the cheating. It's an extreme ego boost for the man who's having sex with another man's woman, and it's extremely detrimental to the ego of her man when he finds out. It's an instant killer to her man's ego and an instant trigger to his pride. The only way for him to bring life back to his ego is to let go of the relationship.

A man cannot live with the fact that his woman had intentions of leaving him for another man. It would also be impossible for a man to eliminate the thoughts of another man having access to his woman mentally and sexually. Even if a man wanted to move past that he wouldn't be able to. His ego-driven thoughts would have him wondering if she felt this other guy was better than him, if the other guy made her feel a way that he couldn't make her feel, and if she's thinking about the other guy while with him. It's not forgivable in a man's eyes because not only is his pride triggered, which affects him internally and how he views himself as a man, but his ego is damaged, which affects him externally and has an impact on how the world views him as a man.

A man has to be number one in the eyes of his woman, the moment another man has the opportunity to take that position, it can no longer be redeemed. Women often misunderstand why a man can't forgive a woman who cheated, even if it were only once. Women always make the comparison to how many times they forgave their man for cheating on them, thinking that would create some type of grounds to stand on for a man to forgive them. Women also think that if the love is strong enough, that should be enough to reconcile and mend the relationship.

I just want to make this very clear; even if a man loves his woman with all his heart, how he feels about her has nothing to do with his inability to forgive her for cheating on him. It's his ego. No amount of love can repair a man's ego once it's damaged, definitely not the love from the woman who damaged it. Truth be told, even if nobody in the world knew a man was cheated on but the people involved, he'd still struggle with accepting it because he'd still know internally, and his pride would prevent him from moving forward with a damaged ego.

Men don't make their decisions contingent upon how they feel. Their decisions are based on rationality in attempts to create the outcome that fits them best. The only thing that can repair a man's ego is time, acceptance, and forgiveness, and in most cases, that forgiveness does not include moving on and staying in the relationship. A damaged ego in a man is a means to an end, but that's not necessarily the case for women. Seeing as though women don't operate from ego, damaging their ego isn't going to write the ending to their relationship, it just may birth some insecurities. Men cannot get past their egos because it's a part of their nature, but men can overcome their pride as long as their ego is not damaged.

Women have strong egos, but their pride is even stronger because it's fueled by their emotions, making it nearly impossible for them to overcome. Why? Because it's in their nature. Men know that emotions are a part of a woman's nature but lack the empathy to truly understand how it factors into who they are. Men aren't always the most compassionate when it comes to a woman's emotions because men are programmed already to operate outside of their own emotions, which makes them assume it not to be a challenge for women.

The truth is, women want to operate outside of their pride and emotions, but it's just as difficult for them as it is for a man to tame his ego. Pride in women is just as important as ego in men. The same way men operate through their ego; women operate completely out of pride; it's just in their nature. A woman's pride does not have to be triggered because she lives in it; it's always activated, so the ultimate objective would be to deactivate a woman's pride.

Men that naturally understand this know that it requires an immense level of kissing up, but that isn't a problem for men because it's in a man's nature not to have pride in his relationship. The presence of a female's pride also allows for a man the opportunity to tap into his soft side and display his ways of making his woman feel special by kissing up, which also strokes his ego, making it an equally yoked exchange.

A woman with pride is never an issue because it's just as much a part of her nature as the ego is a part of a man's nature. Women are constantly battling against a structure within the world that is obsolete, the structure that created a narrative that women are inferior to men. With that being an issue that women are rising above in the world, having a strong sense of pride is very much appropriate because it helps them to put their foot down.

Pride is never the issue; too much pride in an already prideful woman creates the issue. Too much pride in a woman is equivalent to a man with a weak ego, it's dangerous, and a relationship would not be able to survive it. Too much pride in a woman will lead to petty, spiteful, defensive, and vindictive behavior that will go unnoticed as wrongful behavior in her eyes because her pride will wire her to think it's ok.

Remember, too much pride redirects the moral compass and eliminates the boundaries in which the mind will go to protect you after treading unfamiliar territory. Women naturally have it in them to desire new experiences and try new things. Within those desires, they're more subjected to treading unfamiliar territory, thus strengthening their pride as a natural result. A relationship can survive within the natural confines of a woman's pride because a man has just as much of an ability to tend to a woman's pride as she does with his ego. A man will kiss his woman's ass and kiss the ground she walks on, as long as he feels appreciated for his efforts his ego will be satisfied. That exchange from men to women works out perfectly because women love to be treated and appreciated a certain way. Confusion arises when a woman's pride is strengthened over time in a relationship leading to her having expectations.

In a woman's natural desire to experience new things, it's very easy for current experiences to grow old, constantly creating the need for something new. The moment a woman starts to expect from a man, she's setting herself up for a letdown. It doesn't matter what she's expecting, once the expectations start, the appreciation vanishes, and the pride grows stronger.

This eliminates the opportunity for men to naturally make a woman happy because the things that once counted are now expected. Thoughtful text messages, dates, quality time, protecting, and providing goes unappreciated once a woman develops expectations. Women start to view these things as a requirement, that eliminates the value of it. It's ok to become accustomed to these things but also important to still view them as a luxury in consideration of the efforts of a man. The truth is, no man can satisfy a woman with expectations because expectations are subject to change and eventually will grow higher. There's no limit to the height an expectation can grow to, but the higher the expectation, the higher the chance of letdown.

Pride plays a major part in this because the moment a woman feels as though she's not receiving what she wants or feels as though her needs aren't being met, she's not going to meet the needs of her man. Which inevitably will cause turmoil in the relationship. It's natural for a woman to operate out of her pride and want for her efforts to be matched.

154

It's not natural for a man to be capable of matching a woman's efforts if all of his efforts are being measured by her expectations.

Women view their expectations as part of their standards. Expectations are not a part of having standards because standards are created naturally through your moral compass. Pride created expectations and confused them with standards.

Women with a strengthened pride think that by eliminating their expectations, they will be lowering their standards. *"A woman with expectations will always end up with exes." ~ Wolf ~*

If a relationship is to work, a man will have to understand how to live with and tend to his woman's pride. When all is said and done, all women have is their pride, and they have no problem displaying the strength of it, this is why women often get called stubborn. The chances of getting a woman to put her pride aside are slim to none.

Don't believe me? Try to get a woman to apologize for something. Even if she's wrong, she's going to struggle with giving the proper apology. In most cases, I can almost assure you that her apology is going to be conjoined with a "but" before then explaining her actions and why it's not all her fault. A woman's pride is so strong that she can hold onto the smallest grudge for the longest amount of time. A woman's pride will convince her that walking away from her relationship for something minor is the only option, even if she's completely in the wrong, just to avoid apologizing. This behavior is considered petty and is not intended to be truly detrimental to a relationship.

A man is more willing to fight for his relationship when he's wrong and sometimes even when she's wrong as long as it's not damaging to his ego, but a man is not likely to return to a relationship once he exits. A woman is more willing to walk away from her relationship for something small and petty if she doesn't feel she received the proper apology. Still, a woman is also more willing to come back from something big if a man can get her to put her pride aside.

This will take a whole lot of kissing up and reassurance. This is because women don't care how they're viewed by the world, so their ego being damaged isn't that severe, making it easier for them to forgive their man after he cheated as long as there are still grounds to stand on emotionally. As long as no capital behavior occurred, a woman is open to staying in her relationship because it's natural for women to seek understanding. Within that understanding they seek, it provides an opportunity for them to forgive. Grounds for a woman to stand on would mean she's able to justify her man's behavior to herself as well as the public if necessary. If a woman has grounds to stand on, she will still be willing to work things out, as long as a man does his part in reassuring her that no capital behavior was included and that it'll never happen again.

The only issue with that is, women now have convinced themselves through their pride and redirecting of their moral compass that it makes them weak to forgive their man after he stepped out, regardless of how meaningless the experience was. Remember that pride, when triggered, strengthens as a way to protect yourself after treading unfamiliar territory. Which is what creates a redirection of the moral compass. Women are already naturally prideful, and once they are hurt and emotionally confused, they have to recalibrate their entire moral compass to protect themselves and ensure that they are never hurt in that way again. In recalibrating their moral compass, women often reflect on what they did that made them vulnerable and subjected to the pain that was endured. During their reflection, they draw the conclusion that it was a result of them being too understanding and willing to forgive. This is why women that are cheated on will modify their view on them being understanding. It'll go from being a strength to it becoming their biggest weakness. The shift in point of view occurs because being too understanding makes them feel vulnerable and subject to being hurt again.

Most women will refer to themselves as guarded, or they'll say they have their guard up. When a woman puts her guard up, she is attempting to protect herself from any potential opportunities to be hurt, which will heighten her chances of being hurt before it reduces them.

The major problem with that defense is that a woman putting her guard up only protects her from the hurt that looks familiar. It doesn't protect from unfamiliar pain. You can't guard yourself against something you never saw before; this is why women trying to refrain from dealing with certain types of men that may have hurt them, only result in them being hurt in a different way by a "different" man.

Most importantly, a woman guarding herself won't protect her from the pain she causes herself in attempts to protect herself. Then again, women would much rather hurt themselves than allow for a man to hurt them; their pride won't allow it. This strongly developed way of thinking for women has relationships coming to an end abruptly, prematurely, and without reason or proper understanding. Women are now intolerant to any male behavior that appears to resemble the behaviors that resulted in them being cheated on. In hopes of avoiding being cheated on again. This is becoming outrageous and unrealistic because it's affecting every dating experience or relationship they enter.

The lack of tolerance is not the issue. The issue is it being fueled by pride and an uncontrollable redirected moral compass. Women have become so afraid of being hurt again that the expectations they are creating through their moral compass destroy their own happiness. Women now are viewing any form of a man entertaining or displaying any potential interest in another female as "cheating," and it's causing them unnecessary hurt and pain.

Not to say that a woman should be ok with her man displaying an interest in another woman. It's more so to say that it shouldn't be held to the standard of an actual physical cheating encounter with another woman just because it resembles the pattern of something they've experienced in the past.

Eliminating understanding from a woman's mind creates so much chaos within herself that she's unable to rationalize any of her decisions. Why? Because it's in a woman's nature to seek understanding, which soothes her spirit, but her mind is wired to view understanding as a weakness, which is fueled by her pride. Women are now trying to prevent themselves from being hurt by investing more energy and attention into the signs of a man cheating than they do into the efforts of their own happiness.

This is where you see relationships end for reasons that aren't so severe, like a man liking photos of another girl on social media. See, men never view this as an issue, but for women, it's not that liking another woman's photos are an issue, it's how they view the intent from their perspective.

Socializing can lead to fraternizing, which then could lead to cheating, and women don't want that. In their attempts to protect themselves, they are identifying certain behavior early and attempting to stop it in its roots. This method is not necessarily wrong if it were used to fight terminal illness. Still, it's not the most suitable method for a woman protecting herself from getting hurt, or as an attempt to save her relationship. Why? Because it'll appear as if she's overreacting, which will cause fury in a woman and rebellion in a man, which can then make him appear to be disobedient or inconsiderate to the things that she doesn't prefer him to do while in a relationship.

So here we have it, in her attempt to spare herself hurt and pain, she's actually creating chaos and confusion within her relationship, which is helpful to no one. For women to reestablish their level of understanding and take back control of their own happiness, it would require them to put a lot of their pride aside. Men can only operate within the natural nature of a woman's pride. Only a woman can eliminate some of her pride to make herself less prideful. Right now, women are leaving their happiness up to a man by having these expectations and requirements only to be let down when he's unable to measure up to them.

Women can't expect a man to understand how to operate within their moral compass if they don't understand how to operate within their own moral compass. Women have to internalize and identify what occurred that caused the shift in their perspective regarding what makes them vulnerable. Once women can identify what caused the shift, they can revert their moral compass back to its origin of operation and operate by nature and not pride.

Women must also regain their level of understanding within themselves as well as the nature of a man. Understand this, being open to understanding doesn't mean tolerating things that go against the moral compass. It means allowing for yourself the opportunity to gain the clarity needed to rationalize what's acceptable and what's not acceptable. There's no one way for a moral compass to correctly operate, seeing as though everybody's spirit is different, but there is a wrong way, and that is operating out of pride. A woman redirecting her moral compass so that she can revert back to operating inside of her nature is an effective way for her to reclaim her personal power. Having personal power limits the opportunity for a man to hurt her, whether it be intentionally or unintentionally.

That process is beneficial for women because they'll no longer feel the need to guard themselves, which then allows them the opportunity of finding happiness for themselves, with a man and without the fear of being vulnerable or hurt again. Women reverting back to operating inside of their nature with understanding is important for relationships because not only will it give them clarity instead of confusion, it'll eliminate their unrealistic expectations they put on men, or at least minimize them. This allows for a woman to be happy with the efforts of her man. A woman's ability to understand is what helps her rationalize if her relationship is worth it or not in the face of adversity.

Men have to be equally understanding for a relationship to work. Men have to learn, understand, and respect the nature of a woman's pride, and women have to learn, understand, and respect the nature of a man's ego. Neither men nor women can expect one another to respect each other's nature without mutual respect. A man can't expect a woman to respect his ego if he cannot deal with her pride, and a woman can't expect a man to deal with her pride beyond the benefits it serves his ego.

The moral of the story is, a man's ego may drive him to cheat; a woman's pride may drive her away! Don't damage a man's ego and don't trigger a woman's pride.

That is not to say that a man can't have more pride than a woman or a woman can't have an ego that's weaker than a man's, just in more cases than not, it's never the latter. Men want their ego stroked because it provides them with status; women want their ass kissed because of their pride. A man is more likely to cheat behind his ego. He's also more likely to apologize first. Whereas women are less likely to cheat, but it's nearly impossible to get a woman to apologize first because of her pride. His ego will make him do certain things, and her strong pride will not let certain things go. The only solution is understanding.

If men and women can respect each other's nature, they can respect each other. Men and women who understand this tend to have long-lasting relationships that can stand the test of time and turmoil.

Understanding the role played by his ego, and her pride in a relationship is so important. It helps men and women avoid taking everything so personal as if it was directed toward each other when certain things are just a part of a man and woman's nature.

Not taking thing's personal in your relationship will always give extended life to your relationship because it provides you with the ability to be understood, to be understanding, and to be open to forgiveness.

Chapter 11

Should You Forgive?

If you've made it this far into the book, you may have had to take a moment or two to yourself to reflect on some things, forgiveness being one of them. You're probably wondering when and if you should forgive the person that cheated on you.

Make no mistake, just because you forgive your partner, or your partner forgives you doesn't mean the relationship will still be a relationship. In most cases, the relationship is ended, or it becomes a sinking ship in the sea of toxicity, which over time, will still write its own tragic ending. Forgiveness is coming to terms with what happened and deciding to be at peace with it, no longer carrying hate, anger, guilt, or resentment toward anyone.

The problem is most people claim to forgive, but in reality, they haven't, they just made the decision to move on with it still affecting them as opposed to moving on from it. Moving on from a situation can mean staying with your partner, or it can mean forgiving but deciding to move on from your partner and the relationship.

The key to forgiveness, if you decide to move on with your partner, is to understand that you can't carry the situation with you, in any way, shape, form, or fashion. You have to come to terms with what happened and consciously make the decision to let it go. If you don't completely come to terms with being cheated on and you decide to stay, it can only result in toxic behavior, which undoubtedly leads to a toxic relationship.

It's never ok to stay in a relationship if you're going to be toxic or if your partner is toxic. You both may as well just start the breakup process and get a head start on it because that moment is still going to arrive, and you're both still going to have to deal with the emotions associated with moving on.

Partners that decide to stay together in toxicity are afraid of being alone, moving on, or starting over. So, they make the decision to stick around and adapt to living in chaos. Truth is, some people don't even realize they're being toxic and have gotten so accustomed to arguments and fights that it became a part of their relationship routine to mentally and sometimes physically tear each other apart.

The fear of being alone stems from losing your sense of self while in a relationship. It is when you have been so invested into a relationship that you forgot which habits, tendencies and personality traits were your true-self vs. the ones you've developed during your relationship. There's also a high chance of feeling like you've lost your sense of independence. You've gotten so used to sleeping next to someone, having someone to talk to every day, and having someone to call your own that you refuse to let it go in fear of never being the same, or ever finding someone equal to or better than what you currently have.

People in toxic relationships also have a fear of moving on. Moving on means, letting go and that's difficult for people because the results of letting go are unknown. You never know who you'll end up with or who your partner will end up with.

Truthfully, more of people's fear of moving on come from who their partner will end up with as opposed to who they'll end up with. In most cases, it's easier to see someone else moving on before you see yourself moving on, those thoughts create a fear which makes people want to hold on to their relationship.

The biggest and most terrifying fear associated with why people stay in toxic relationships is the fear of starting over. The thought of starting over makes people feel like the relationship was all for nothing or a waste of time, and if you know, one thing people hate to waste is their time. Starting over also means trying again, which is hard for people because they fear the possibilities of getting the same results in their next relationship. No one wants to take the time to regather themselves, enter the dating world, meet a total stranger, start the process of getting to know one another, develop a connection and then become spouses, all for it to potentially result in the same outcome. It sounds like too much just reading it, Ha-ha-ha.

Also, take into account that humans create routines, and if they could, they would live in those routines forever, rarely making any changes worth noting. So, having to break those routines and then create new ones tend to make people choose to stay rather than to leave, even if it means dealing with a little toxicity.

"I mean, what's a relationship without toxicity?" I've often heard people say that, because, in today's society, toxicity is mistaken for love. One tip to my readers: Don't hate yourself so much to a point where you find normality in toxicity.

Furthermore, to forgive and stay in a relationship as with anything is circumstantial, and those circumstances measure differently in the eyes of each individual based on their moral compass. It's important not to judge but instead to be understanding.

If you are in a relationship and you are cheated on, always ask yourself if your pain is coming from your pride and ego or if it's truly affecting you by going against your moral compass. Doing so will help you to rationalize if you can forgive and stay in your relationship or if you should move on from it.

A deal-breaker in one relationship can be a test of strength in another relationship. I learned that for some people, meaningless sex isn't a deal-breaker depending on what they have invested and what they stand to lose. Some relationships are a partnership, so sex isn't that big a deal. A person in a partnership-based relationship with kids, a mortgage, a car note, and combined bank accounts with their spouse may look at a sex affair as a dent in the armor of the relationship. Still, that's not enough to cut all ties to the relationship because their relationship isn't based on intimacy; it's based on partnership.

Does that mean that two people in a partnership-based relationship don't genuinely love each other? No, it doesn't; it means their love for the totality of their relationship stretches far beyond the intimacy aspect of it. On the other hand, a person in a relationship with a base of intimacy could look at an affair as extremely detrimental to the relationship and may view it as unforgivable even if they have those same things invested as the person in the partnership-based relationship. Why? Because sex is held to a higher standard in a relationship based on intimacy. In neither case is either point of view wrong, it just proves how people measure the same things differently. If you ask me, I think it's easier to forgive being cheated on and to stay in a relationship involving manslaughter than it is when it involves capital behavior.

Still, I've witnessed certain situations where capital behavior was forgiven. I think whichever decision you decide to make should come down to an honest conversation with yourself on if it's someone you will be better off living with or living without based on your moral compass and the love you two share.

It's important not to make an emotional-based decision. If your emotions are high, then take some time away before coming to your conclusion. You should never make your decision based on your emotional state because your decision will be irrational whether you decide to stay in the relationship or to leave it.

Too many relationships where two people were destined to be together ended due to cheating. It's unfortunate because there's a high chance it could've easily been worked out. There are also too many relationships with people that are drowning in toxicity from cheating that should've been ended, but they're afraid to let go. If you know it'll hurt you more to stay, then leave the relationship. If you know, it'll hurt you more to leave, then work it out. Just make sure the decision you make is the decision you can live with, and it involves forgiveness.

Chapter 12

How to Forgive

I'll start by saying this; it takes a lot of strength and courage to forgive someone who has wronged you, especially someone you love and trust. I feel as though there are three elements of forgiveness.

Forgive you, forgive them and for some people, forgive the situation to move forward together. Forgiving starts with forgiving you, as easy as it sounds; it's not the easiest thing for people to do. It's actually easier for someone to forgive others than it is for them to forgive themselves. Why? Because it's much easier to impose self-blame, and it gives an immediate answer providing closure to the situation.

The faster we can gain closure, the easier it is to move on from the situation, the only issue with that is, all closure isn't the closure it takes to heal from a hurtful and traumatic situation.

Self-blame does nothing to contribute to our healing process. It actually works against us by putting us into a state of denial. The real reason closure is so important to us is because we, as humans, have a burning desire to gain an understanding of what happened, we have a need to know. We want answers even if they're not the truth. We want to know when it started, why you did it, what we could've done differently to prevent it, and so on. That need to know creates a feeling of emptiness inside of us when that void is not filled with answers.

On the other side of that need to know, we also have a fear of rejection and a fear of not getting the answers or responses that we want. This fear creates a mental battle within us consisting of when and if we will ever get the closure we so desperately desire from the person who has caused us pain. Since no one wants to wait for something, they're not guaranteed ever to get it usually results in self-blame.

Let's be honest; when something bad happens to us, we want to put it behind us as quickly as possible and move on from it so we can continue on with our lives. With that being said, it's much easier to take the blame rather than to ask the culprit and allow room for a response we don't want, wasn't expecting or worst! No answer at all. It is much easier to look karma in the face and say, "I brought this on myself," or, "I deserved it for not being a better spouse," as opposed to facing the culprit.

The truth is, we can't prevent someone from cheating on us, nor can we prevent them from doing anything to us that may cause us pain. Even with that being the truth, it doesn't stop us from putting ourselves at fault and making ourselves the blame for their actions.

Look at it this way; if you're at an intersection crossing the street on your green light, and get hit by a car that ran through the red light, it won't make sense for you to say, "it's my fault for crossing the street on a green light before double-checking to make sure no insane driver was going to run a red light." In that situation, although you may feel you could've done more to prevent it, the truth is you did everything you were supposed to do, and it still happened. That's the way you should view being cheated on because, in both cases, your rightful actions didn't prevent their wrongful actions. The actions of another human being are not in our control, so there's no benefit in us holding ourselves accountable for, or making ourselves the cause of their actions. People are going to do what they want to do, and we can't stop them.

In all reality, there's no long-term benefit in taking the blame for something you didn't do, but there are long-term effects of possible hate, anger, guilt, or resentment toward yourself and the situation.

Yes, you gain an immediate response, which may feel good and convince you that your healing process is starting, but it doesn't start there, you can't free yourself of anything until you make peace with it. The healing process doesn't start until you find forgiveness in yourself for yourself. Doing so is how you create that peace for all that has happened, allowing yourself to be healed from it.

Forgiving yourself isn't asking you to ignore what happened or how it affected you; it's allowing yourself to let go of the pain so you can heal completely. Forgiveness allows you to free yourself of any anger, guilt, hurt, or resentment toward the situation in its entirety. Carrying those emotions prevents you from progressively growing, and it gives the situation power over you.

To strip the situation of the power it has over you, you must release all of the negative emotions associated with it, not somewhat, and not partially, you must eradicate them by forgiving yourself. Do not confuse forgiving yourself with blaming yourself.

185

Blaming yourself is saying, "it's my fault," which creates self-hate while forgiving yourself is saying, "I know it's not my fault, but I will not allow anger, guilt or resentment to travel with me as I move away from this situation" which is showcasing self-love.

We cannot control what has happened to us, but we can control how long we allow it to affect us by carrying negative emotions toward it. The moment you make the decision to forgive yourself is the moment you regain your peace of mind, your personal power, and you allow yourself to move on while developing a level of strength you didn't realize was in you.

So, forgive yourself not to take the accountability of someone else's actions but instead to display the amount of love you have for yourself by not wanting to suffer any longer. There's no right or wrong amount of time to arrive at forgiving yourself, but the sooner, the better if you want to stop your personal suffering.

After successfully forgiving yourself, you will be able to forgive the person or people that caused you the pain. I assure you that it's impossible to forgive yourself and still hold anger toward someone else. If you claim to have forgiven yourself but didn't find it in you to forgive them, you don't truly forgive yourself, and all you did was put the blame on them.

Forgiveness isn't about who's to blame; it's more about everyone individually taking responsibility for their own mercy. As absurd as it may sound, the culprit isn't supposed to wait for you to forgive them just as you shouldn't wait for them to give you closure. Their healing process is no different than yours, they would have to forgive themselves for what they've done, and you would have to forgive yourself if you want to free yourself of the pain and suffering it caused you.

With everyone focusing on forgiveness, no negative emotions are being carried toward the situation, which will successfully allow it to be left in the past. It's not for us to punish someone for their actions by wanting revenge or wanting them to suffer the same pain they've caused us. If we want them to experience the pain we have suffered, then we aren't healed. Every thought of them suffering is actually punishing ourselves because, to develop those thoughts, we would still have to be hurting from what happened.

Don't view forgiveness as letting someone else off the hook, view it as freeing yourself. You will know if you're successfully healed from a situation or if you truly forgive someone when you see how you react when their name or the situation is brought up, or the thoughts you develop when you think about them and the situation.

If your thoughts are still negative and your reaction is still with anger, guilt, or resentment, then you aren't entirely healed. Being hurt creates wounds. Although they aren't always displayed on your physical body, the pain isn't any less severe, and in most cases, it's worse.

Look at it this way, just like with wounds to your flesh, over time they heal, and although they're still there, the pain you once felt is gone once it completely heals. A knee scrape you acquired as a child shouldn't still be causing you pain as an adult, even if the wound is still visibly there. Yes, I know a knee scrape isn't as severe as being cheated on, but the concept is the same and even if I were to replace scraping your knee with cutting your leg open and needing stitches, over time that wound is still going to heal, and the pain is still going to go away.

The same goes for the events that wound our mental. The wound is still there, but once we are completely healed, the pain is going to go away, and it won't hurt to touch on the topic. Forgiving is not forgetting; it is letting go and freeing yourself. It is not to say that what happened didn't happen, but to say that I am healed, and although my wounds may have made me who I am, they do not define who I am.

Now I will say this, forgiveness plays a pivotal role in your personal growth, and after you heal, you'll be able to determine if you're moving on from the situation alone or with your partner to work things out.

It takes a lot of strength to forgive and twice as much power to arrive at the decision to work things out, but it's always worth it in the end.

Chapter 13

Things to Take with You

If you've made it this far into the book, congratulations! But before you put the book down, there are some things you must understand!

Cheating is not cheating. There's no universal law that identifies cheating in apparent fact; in fact, cheating is subjective, perspective, and circumstantial. The determination of what is considered cheating has to be established by those involved in the relationship, and no one else!

Too many relationships are ending due to the opinions of others. Do not allow someone else to convince you to love the way they love nor hurt the way they hurt because, in doing so, you will only love-less and hurt more. Live and walk in your truth. Your truth is your happiness. If your truth is to result in pain, then at least it's your pain to walk in and heal from. As opposed to some unidentifiable pain created and caused by the views of society.

There's no need to follow the criteria established by society as to what should be considered cheating because the opinion of society will never be more valid than your own opinion. Society has created an illusion that women can change the nature of a man, even by changing the nature of themselves, which is a lie and, as a result, caused the natural balance of relationships to be completely off.

You hear it all the time; "A man will be a man" It's been that way and always will be that way. Society has also created an illusion that a woman will find a man that she will have entirely to herself, which is true. Still, society isn't emphasizing the fact that that's not going to stop him from stepping out with other women if that's what he wants to do to satisfy his ego.

This takes us back to intent being a key factor in how a cheating situation should be viewed. Men and women have two totally different perspectives and viewpoints when it comes to cheating, and those differences stem from their nature. The moral of the story is, society has created illusions that have tampered with reality. If relationships are to last, they'll have to operate inside of reality, but that doesn't mean you can't get your fairytale ending.

Everyone wants a relationship that lasts forever, but none of us knows what forever looks like or what it'll take to make it to forever. We often ignore the potential for adversity, turmoil, and problems that occur over time no matter what's going on in your life. People have it fixated in their minds that love is supposed to create the perfect ending. Just because it ends perfectly doesn't mean there weren't any problems that had to be overcome in the middle. Think about all of the fairytales with a storybook ending. There was some type of problem that arose that had to be overcome to get to the happy ending. Most people skip from the beginning to end, not knowing that it's what's in the middle that determines how the ending will play out.

Truth is reality, and reality is the truth! It's important to operate inside of reality, but it's more important to operate inside of the reality in which you created for yourself based on what makes you happy. Society can't tell you what or who makes you happy, trying to rely on that will always leave you unhappy, confused, and feeling empty. It's easy to identify what makes you happy because it's naturally soothing to your spirit, it feels like your soul's cravings are being satisfied, and as a result, you'll feel fulfilled. I wrote this book to help identify the importance of intent, understanding, forgiveness, and healing. We must understand these things to have long-lasting successful relationships with ourselves and with others.

I also wrote this book as a guide to help women and men develop an understanding of one another. I wanted to help men and women understand themselves, the role they play in their relationship, and how that role impacts the success or demise of the relationship. A man who cannot understand himself will always struggle to find a comfortable place in his relationship, which will derive more insecurities and a weaker ego, thus leading him to cheat. A woman who cannot understand herself will have more expectations than standards and more confusion than reason. Leaving her always to feel incomplete, unhappy, and like she's missing something, even if she has it right in front of her face.

A man who cannot understand the nature of a woman will lack the empathy, compassion, and respect for her emotions and her process, thus creating a disconnect leading to her feeling undervalued and unappreciated outside of the things she does for him. This will subject her to seeking it in another man. A woman who cannot accept and respect a man's nature will always find herself incapable of dealing with his ego and, in more cases than not, will result in her damaging it.

The most important element to a successful relationship is respect! Not just respect for one another or respect for one's self, but the respect of each other's nature. Women have to respect a man's ego, it's a part of him, and no matter how much a woman tries to destroy it, he will find a way to rebuild it, and she'll only ruin her own relationship. Men have to respect a woman's emotions and pride! No matter how much a man tries to make a woman repress, suppress, or refrain from operating within them, there's no eliminating them.

A man or woman who fails to respect nature will fail to accept love. A relationship without this level of understanding and respect will not be able to survive the test of time and turmoil. Relationships don't end from the problems inside of the relationship. They end from the problems outside of the relationship. An established understanding and a sound foundation are the only things that can stop a relationship from sinking.

If things are not to work in your relationship, then forgiveness and healing are equally essential to understand, and just as vital to living in your reality. There's no need to punish yourself or others for things that don't go as planned. No need to feel like you're the recipient of some sort of love curse or that love is just not on your side.

Learn to take from every situation what serves you and leave behind everything that doesn't. A relationship that comes to an end isn't always a failed relationship; it may have just run its course. Some people are placed in our lives to improve us for ourselves or for the next person, and we are placed in people's lives for the same reason.

It's important also not to judge yourself or others, learn what you love, and how to love what you love. Also, learn to love what others love, even if it's not the love for you. You do not have to live with a love that is not for you! You only have to respect it. The only love you have to live with is the one you create for your reality, whether you're in a relationship with someone or in a relationship with yourself.

Do not block your own blessings by holding on to things, people, and experiences that don't serve you or add value to your reality. The best part about living in your reality is, it's yours! Which means nobody can take it from you, change or alter it without your consent. What's even better than that is you can at any moment decide to create the reality you want to live in!

So, let's do it! Let's create the reality of our desires and eliminate any and all things that tamper with our healing process. Let's remove any and everything that keeps us in bondage with our hurt and our pain so we can free ourselves. Let's restore ourselves so that we can be ready for the love we desire, the love that matches our reality!

Most importantly, let's deprive society of the power it has over our views with our lives, and how we view relationships! There's someone out there for everyone, and we must be open and ready to love and be loved.

Printed in Dunstable, United Kingdom